Shards of Time

MITOS SUSON

DEDICATION

*This book is dedicated to my Dad
who lived by the code of "No guts, no glory!"
This same code inspired me to
follow my dreams fearlessly.
Thanks, Dad.*

CONTENTS

PROLOGUE
MY JOURNEY

Who am I?

I was plagued with this question from the moment I could start thinking for myself.

My name is Mita Zara and having lived half a century and more, my life still revolves around this question.

My journey started on the day I was born, although sometimes, I suspect it even began long before that. I was born on a Sunday in the Sixties, of a God-fearing religious family. After my mother gave birth to four boys, my parents were delighted at the arrival of a girl. My birth was such a joyful sweetness to my parents that they were compelled to call me Carmelitos meaning "Candy" or also "Sweetie" for short.

I was born on a Palm Sunday, the season when Jesus entered Jerusalem, the crowd welcoming him with palms and branches from their native trees. Since then, it was celebrated every year by most Catholic countries at the start of the Lenten season to prepare forty days of fasting, abstinence, or sacrifice depicting Christ's forty days in the desert before Easter Sunday celebration. Religious convictions overruled and I was named Pamita, Mita for short. Only the name Maria was registered on my birth certificate. That was not uncommon for Filipinos to christen their daughters with the first name Maria, after the Blessed Virgin Mary; almost every third Filipina has acquired the name Maria, so helping to secure their slot in heaven.

After all, what is in a name? I was named after a branch of a tree, but I wish I was named after an edible sweet candy or be like the Virgin Mary, any of those options. The latter was a hard act to follow so I decided to embrace my name Mita which means 'Myth' in Greek. Since then, my entire life's goal was to unravel that myth to reveal my true purpose.

1 SIGNS

It was the summer of 2010; I'm half a century old. I fled from an abusive husband. I abandoned our lovely waterfront home in Benicia and temporarily sought shelter in the woodsy area of Moraga, California until I knew what to do with my life.

God, what is wrong with me? Condemning myself for a second failed marriage. I thought I had it all after ingesting a litany of self-help books.

Unlike my first marriage when I blamed myself for my twenty-two-year-old youth and naiveté, the recent divorce was more difficult for me, because there was more than a ten-year interim before I consciously embarked on a second marriage at forty-two-years old. Through numerous therapy sessions and DIY self-help books, I worked on improving myself and genuinely believed that I had evolved into a better human being. I felt like a dismal failure.

When will I ever learn? I asked myself while sitting on the bed and folding laundry, loathing myself to the core.

I remember having responded to a room rental ad on Craigslist,

Female roommate wanted – Fully furnished pet-friendly room in a beautiful townhouse, excellent location. Rent includes all utilities, cable TV, internet. Must live with a cat. References required.

I reached out immediately to the contact number published in the ad, to secure the first available appointment.

Moments later, I was in my car with Z, my gold and a tan furball of a Yorkie on my lap; his paws on the wheel. I stepped on the gas upon reaching 780 East, merging into CA 24 East freeway from Benicia in Northern California, and exiting at Moraga Road. I drove through a threshold of trees following a winding mountainous terrain.

I prayed, "Lord, please guide me through. Is this the right decision? Please send me a sign."

To my dismay, I stepped on the breaks as a deer family sprung from one side of the road to the opposite direction. The world stopped and I was lost in a trance by their magnificence and glory. A fawn trailed behind the mother deer followed by a strong proud majestic buck with massive, splendid antlers. The buck stopped and looked at me with a prolonged gaze, our eyes locked.

'*Welcome to Moraga*', his eyes beckoned me. '*This is where you belong.*'

Breathless and astounded by his beauty and proud strut, I considered it a sign. I thrived on signs.

Being alone propelled me to cultivate my intuition and act upon the signs and symbols the universe would send my way. As I drove further, this confirmed I was headed toward the right path.

I turned off the aircon and rolled the windows down. A gush of wind swept the hair away from my face. Z popped his head out of the window and basked in the summer breeze with the wind blowing his golden tresses. The road was studded with pines and all sorts of trees. I drew in the enigmatic energy from the trees and nature; I was enveloped by its glory. I loved it here, the air felt different.

Revitalized by the trees, a painful memory broke my reverie. I had run away from home to the ends of the earth to erase a tragic past. A tight knot formed in my chest reminding me of the pristine waters and palm trees of Cebu, Philippines, an island in the Far East where I grew up, realizing I have the soul of an island girl in exile. Tears trickled down my cheeks spelling how homesick I felt. Sinking in a melancholic mood I whispered to myself, *Cebu, hang in there; I am coming home soon.*

"You have arrived," the GPS announced. I wiped the tears away from my face and stepped out of the car, clinging to Z.

The townhouse had an English country-like ambiance like it had just graced the cover of a Town and Country magazine. It was a fair-sized two-story house protected by an enclave of trees in one of the exclusive high-end neighborhoods in a town right next to the country club. The house was close to the freeway, in a secluded wooded area next to a brook where the burble of a stream drowned the sounds of the cars. A private walking path led to a golf course. In front of the house was one of my favorite trees, a willow tree. *A second sign.*

The willow tree greeted me by spreading its graceful arching branches as it swayed in the direction of the breeze and danced for me. A plump squirrel clasping a hazelnut scurried along the branches. Z immediately ran to the base of the tree surrounded by the green manicured grass, and before I could stop him, he marked his spot.

"Eww Z, what am I going to do with you?"

He gave me his infamous cute head tilt from left to right, which confirmed I couldn't be mad at him too long.

I approached the entrance, signaling my arrival with the knob of the brass door knocker, then waited.

A middle-aged slender and tall Caucasian lady sporting a blonde French bob, wearing a classic maroon cardigan and jeans, greeted me as she opened the door. Striking silver jewelry decked with Swarovski crystals highlighted her somewhat pale, pretty face.

"Hi, I am Mita and this is Z." I stretched out my hand.

She broke into a smile as soon as she saw Z then gave me a tight handgrip. With her deep and pleasant voice, she said, "Nice to meet you, Mita. My name is Daphne. Come in."

I trailed behind her.

"May I?" Daphne stroked Z's forehead as we headed inside.

I nodded. Z was an icebreaker. Everywhere I went, people would smile at me and say, "That's a cute dog you've got!" And before I knew it, I had made new friends.

Daphne warmed up to me, as we walked inside. "I used to have a dog too. His name was Benjie." Her smile disappeared. "He passed on, a couple of months ago. He had cancer. I paid $18,000 for the surgery, but he still died."

"I am so sorry," I said, seeking the right words to comfort her.

"The vet gave me a loan which I'm still paying," she continued. "He was my best friend, and he was worth every cent."

After an exchange of casual pleasantries, Daphne briefly toured me around the house. A spacious living room was on the right side from the entrance, with a modular sectional sofa facing the 48" widescreen TV. Perpendicular to the sofa was a huge glass window, which showcased the willow tree and the stream.

The living room was connected to the dining room, which led through a glass door to the private garden. The dining area was adjacent to the kitchen forming an L-shaped. An island separated the living room from the kitchen.

Approaching the pantry, Daphne opened the fridge, "You can store your food here."

The fridge was empty except for numerous open bottles of wine, some sealed. We traversed to the living room, where a stairway led to the 2nd floor.

"I live here upstairs with my cat, Chester," Daphne said, as we ascended the stairs.

There were 2 more bedrooms with a shared bathroom. The cat litter was in the hallway between the 2 bedrooms in front of the toilet. Daphne occupied the master bedroom.

We went downstairs and on the right side next to the stairway was the advertised room.

Daphne opened the door of the bedroom, which was a good-sized (30 square feet) cheerful, warm and cozy room. An antique rustic desk nestled in the corner of the room next to the door. A classical vintage French daybed accented with golden brass wrought iron stood out on the opposite end of the room.

"Hope it will be comfortable enough," she sat on the mattress and bounced on it, "it's a brand-new mattress."

Huge windows were right next to the bed, facing the willow and the brook. The room was painted in different shades of blue, emanating warmth and safety. The furnishings were a fusion of country and modern design, blending in harmony.

Peering outside the window, I spotted the beautiful scenery outside with the willow tree and the stream as if depicted in a painting. A wave of a déjà vu' moment washed upon me and every blade of grass, every cell of the trees, and all the pebbles in the stream, reinforced that I had been here a thousand years ago.

My heart pounded while cold chills crept all over my body. I reached out to a chair for balance, then prayed. *Lord, is this another sign?*

Moments later, Daphne led me to a narrow hallway, which also functioned as a mini walk-in closet, that led to the bathroom.

"You will really love the bathroom," Daphne boasted. "I just remodeled it."

Still lost in a trance, the energy continued to welcome me home. Indeed, it was my favorite room in the house.

We stepped inside a spacious private bathroom. There was no bathtub, but a huge luxurious walk-in shower with strong water and modern high-tech jet showers distributed evenly against the walls. Opposite the shower room was a vanity with a large mirror that occupied half the wall making the room larger than it seemed. The sink and the countertops were of the finest marble finish. A door from the bathroom door led to the laundry room.

"You are welcome to do laundry here," she offered.

The laundry room had two doors that led to a private garden facing the street.

After the tour, Daphne asked, "Do you care for some coffee?"

"Sure," I said, feeling incredibly positive about the space.

A strong coffee aroma wafted into the living room where we sat. Daphne reached out for her beautiful China from the cupboard, then poured coffee. Her frail thin hands shook, and she spilled some coffee on the thick original Afghan carpet.

"Dang! Sorry. I just had the carpets cleaned, but the stain would not go away," Daphne apologized.

"Don't worry about it," I assured her. "It does not bother me."

Fidgeting with her hands, and with uneven breaths, Daphne stuttered, "I was diagnosed with Melanoma, but now it's in remission. This is the reason why I need a roommate. My mother died last year, and I quit my job to take care of her. The rent will definitely alleviate some bills."

"I am so sorry," I said, grasping for the right comfort words. "If I could help, it would be great," I shared. "I need a temporary respite while waiting for my divorce to finalize."

We exchanged histories while savoring the coffee.

Moments later, Daphne shut the question, "When are you going to move in?"

A smile played on my lips. I realized I had just passed the interview.

"Tomorrow!" I confirmed. Relieved and jubilant at the same moment, I wanted to jump for joy, but instead, I whispered a prayer. *Thank you, Lord.*

She asked. "Do you need any help? I have a truck."

"That would be great!" I was grateful since I only had a compact sportscar.

"I can drive you to the doctors too for your appointments," I offered.

The seed of a new friendship was sown. Little did I know that Daphne would be instrumental in my new beginnings. Since I needed a place to incubate and without her knowledge, she helped me overcome my depression and recalibrate a new life goal.

***

Several weeks after I settled in my new room and in between coffee and wine exchanges with Daphne, I learned more about her life and family. Her ancestors came from Baton Rouge, Louisiana.

One lazy rainy weekend, when I took a break from work and decided to chill and hang out at home, I spotted Daphne slouched in an armchair, watching her favorite CSI program on TV.

"Hi, Daphne. How's it going? I just bought some wine. Do you care for a glass?" I asked.

"Sure," Daphne said. "Do you want to watch CSI with me? It just started."

"I would love to." I set the hors d'oeuvres—cheese, salami, crackers, salad, and a bottle of wine on the coffee table.

After watching the series, we lingered around in the living room, sharing bits and pieces about ourselves, working on our 2nd bottle.

"When my father passed away, my mother remarried and moved to California with my stepfather who was a successful real estate investor," Daphne revealed. "My mother had the foresight to buy a simple oceanfront cottage in Monterey, CA in the sixties. The value of the property tripled, and she made millions on the sale. She immediately bought two townhouses here in Moraga. The other house was two hundred meters to the west from here, a few minutes' walk away. The entire golf course was her backyard."

"Wow! Lucky you," I said.

"My father was also born in the Philippines," she added.

I said, "What a small world. Who would have expected that you had ties to the Philippines?"

"My grandfather had a publishing company in Manila right after World War II." Daphne rose from the chair, approached the shelf, and pulled out a photo album that exhibited vintage photos of her ancestors in Manila during the 1800s.

She plopped herself on the couch and we perused the pictures.

"Amazing." I studied the sepia-colored photographs of her family and Manila. "Manila looks very different now."

We both nodded.

As our friendship blossomed, our daily schedules also complimented each other. Daphne had insomnia and she slept late at night watching TV and guzzling wine, barely eating. She would wake up by noon or sometimes later. I started my day early, usually at 5:00 AM after Z's first yip, and retired to bed at 9:00 PM. We rarely got into each other's way, but we both knew the company was available if needed.

2 NOSTALGIA

July 2010

My morning rituals involved a spiritual practice, a fusion of religions revisited from the beliefs explored, retained, which resonated with me. From Buddhism to a pinch of Hinduism, a folkloric touch leaning towards Spiritism, and a tad of Christianity, they were mine. I retained my innate Catholicism which is deeply ingrained in my system. I acknowledged Jesus Christ as my Lord and Savior, but also considered him as my personal mystical friend and spirit guide.

Settling into a routine in my new habitat, my day often started with a meditation at the break of dawn. The moon faded. The sun emerged. I lit a patchouli incense at my homemade altar in one corner of my room. The mood spelled stillness, except for the chirping of the birds and the faint howl of the dogs from a distance.

"Om…" I sat upright on the floor, in the middle of the room with my legs crossed in a lotus position, eyes closed, both hands flowed to the opposite side of each knee, palms faced upward as my thumb touched the middle finger forming a circle, in prep for meditation and prayer.

"Om…" the mantra reverberated in my system and awakened every cell in my body, while I sunk slowly into a trance.

I zoned in on my breathing. Inhaling from my nose, as my stomach expanded and exhaled from my mouth. I pumped my tummy in and out, cleansing my internal organs with my breath until a rhythmic flow settled upon me. I opened my eyes and glanced at the clock. At 5:30 AM, Z licked my knees vying for my attention. Deep in the blessed stillness, I ignored his attempts.

"Yip," Z's yelp pierced right into my solemn moment.

"Yip," Z chirped persistently, knowing that his shrill ring tone would eventually strike a chord into my nerves, confident it would trigger a reaction. Like a synced clock, Z barked indicating, "Breakfast, mommy love! Z is hungry."

Z seemed to have his internal clock, and I have not needed an alarm since I've had him. Every morning, we battle constantly over time.

I untangled my pose and rose from the floor, uncurled myself from a hunchback position, lifted my shoulders first, spine, vertebrae after vertebrae, neck, and raised my head until I was in an upright position.

Meditation always rejuvenated me, and I needed this quiet time, where I invoked my higher power and set my intentions for me, my loved ones, and the entire universe. After an hour of communion with the divine, I was awake, refreshed, and energized with a clear mind. Lately, these moments have been my lifeline as I struggled with depression, drowning in helplessness and defeat.

After meditation, I grabbed Z and stepped out of the house to go on a hike. We followed the pathway of the creek. It led us to the peripherals of the golf course. When we hiked, we were enshrouded with the early fog mist, and a family of deer greeted us to welcome the day.

Working up a sweat while hiking the mini hills and valleys, along the course, I thought to myself, *a good dog is a tired dog.* I loved our daily walks which gave me ample time to collect my thoughts. At that moment, I was thinking of my current timetable. It was mid-November 2010, and the holidays were approaching. After an hour, we rested on a secluded spot under a fig tree.

With Thanksgiving scheduled with friends next week, the holidays compelled me to check on Dad. I was worried about him. He had not been the same since Mom passed away twelve years ago in 1998. She was only sixty-seven years old. This triggered memories of my last visit to Cebu.

Cebu is a tiny, elongated strip of an island in the center of the Philippines and surrounded by hundreds of other islands in different shapes and sizes. It is the second capital after Metro Manila, which was discovered by Portuguese explorer Ferdinand Magellan in 1521. On that day, he baptized Rajah Humabon and his queen, the tribal king of Cebu, as well as eight hundred more Filipinos. Thus, Cebu earned the title "Asia's Cradle of Christianity."

Due to its strategic location Cebu maintains a busy port, which has made it a prosperous and flourishing town. Despite being a tiny cosmopolitan city, Cebu has retained its unique island charm. This is the reason why expats, investors, and even Filipinos from different islands have migrated here. It's rich culture and heritage has given pride to every Cebuano, which includes my family.

My sister Candy used to work in the airlines. As an airline employee, our parents could avail for free family passes. Dad luxuriously came and went, as if he just hopped into an airbus from Cebu to San Francisco, in first class seats. He visited us twice a year to see his doctors and take advantage of his Medicare plan. He also flew to the United States to maintain his green card before its validity expired. It was a good excuse to spend some time and hang out with us. Even so, no one could persuade Dad to move to the US because he loved being in the comforts of his own home.

Without any warning, Dad called for a family reunion in 2008. It was never my intention to visit because all my life, I'd been running away from home. I avoided any reason to relive our past. But when your old man calls, who are we to disagree? Out of the blue, he needed to see all his children around him.

I was transported back to that fateful reunion.

Coming home after several years was indeed bittersweet. Dust filled my nostrils as I scanned each room, swallowing hard as the ghosts of the past overtook the present. *Why did I have to come back?* Our home had deteriorated—the paint on the walls chipped off, the toilets clogged and there were boxes strewn in the living room.

Dinner was set, and my siblings and I were all at the dining table catching up while waiting for Dad. He popped out of the room and stood 5"4 tall, ideal weight for his medium frame. His sleek, glossy, jet-black hair preserved his youth, and he smelled like he always did, of Old Spice aftershave.

My heart sank as Dad limped toward us; his left leg impaired from a recent stroke. Other than the decline of his mobility skills, Dad still looked good at eighty-years-old.

"Dad, let's get rid of these boxes," I suggested. "You might trip on it."

"What boxes?" He raised his eyebrows.

Was he in denial?

I approached Mom's piano in the living room and envisioned her presence playing her favorite melody from *Mozart, Bach, and Beethoven*. She was, elegant and smiling with her fair-skinned, dark ebony hair teased in a beehive bun. Her huge hazel-brown almond eyes, thick eyebrows, naturally long lashes, and thick pouty lips accentuated her beauty. Her smile was her best accessory. She'd smiled at her problems, through good times and bad. She dressed in the 60s fashion showing off her wasp-shaped curves. Mom was hot! When she played the piano, she was transported to another realm. She was totally in her element. Mom definitely rocked the piano.

Shortly after, bile rose in my throat as I ran my fingers on the keyboard. The piano was out of tune, with faded keys that stood through time but had seen better days. This was mom's piano, and she would be furious to see it at its current state.

Like the piano, our house was in shambles. I closed my eyes visualizing when Mom was alive. A warm sensation penetrated my chest. Potted plants and flowers strategically planted all over the house breathe fragrant vibrant energy. Bright and colorful curtains depicted springtime, and the house was spotlessly clean. *Our house was a home.* I opened my eyes not wanting to face the reality that Mom was gone, and without her, the house turned gray like winter; dull, dark, dinghy, and dirty. The house deteriorated into a lifeless termite-infested skeletal structure.

Z nudged my leg morphing me back to reality in Moraga. With Dad's recent stroke, his visits to the US were less frequent. Although I was not ready to face my demons, I worried about his health, and this prompted me to make that call. "C'mon Dad, pick up." I clasped my grip on the iPhone visualizing him eighty-one-year-old, small frame, salt and pepper hair, tiny face with a narrow jaw, bulging slanted eyes, straight edge nose, and garbed in his white sando and shorts. Its 6:00 PM, Cebu time. I bet he was slouched on the sofa from his bedroom, watching the daily news. He thrived on *Super-balita* on Channel 7, ABS-CBN which was his window to the world.

"Hello," Dad finally checked in with a strong, clear, but a raspy voice.

"Hey, Dad! It's me, Mita." I pictured his smile from the other end.

"Oy, Mita! When are you coming home?" Dad asked.

"Soon," I promised. "Let me just celebrate Thanksgiving here, Dad, and I'll secure a ticket next week."

"*Sigue lang.* Just make sure you are home for Christmas. Let me know when you are arriving so I can pick you up at the airport," Dad said.

"Just wait for me, Dad, okay?" I pleaded. "Don't do anything crazy. We'll go to Comey Island together."

Comey Island was our sacred space. It is a lush, remote cluster of little islands, North of Cebu, and Dad's birthplace. When we both felt the need to recharge and relax, we would always go back to our source and roots, commune with nature, and bask in the energy of the ocean, rugged roads, palm trees, and the simplicity of the fisher village. We always came out rejuvenated.

"Yes," Dad confirmed, his voice quivering. "As soon as you get back, we'll go to Comey Island," And then there was a quiet pause. The sadness and the loneliness of an old solitary man enveloped me.

"Hang in there, Dad." I clenched the iPhone. "I love you."

After we ended our conversation, I held the phone tight to my chest, right on my heart. Tears trickled down my cheeks. *I miss you, Dad.* Z snuggled close to my neck and licked my tears reminding me that it was time to leave. Taking a deep breath, I rose from the ground, studying the majestic surroundings, but still hoping to get on the plane in two weeks' time.

3 THE PHONE CALL

November 2010

I peered outside the window admiring the ash brown leaves of the red oak tree acknowledging that we were in the midst of the fall season, and the approaching advent of our busiest time at the industrial business park area of Benicia, California. A stack of boxes filled the desk, reminding me of the magic wands I must ship before the end of the day. The phones were ringing off the hook and I was in dire need of my adrenaline rush.

Pressing line one, I sighed. "Thank you for calling."

"When is our package coming?" a customer demanded.

"Do you have a tracking number?"

Line 2 was beeping. "Will it arrive before Christmas? "It's an incredibly special gift, you know. It can't be late!"

Help, I am drowning!

Abby, my boss, and my best friend approached my cubicle. She towered above me at 6"2 tall; she tucked her ginger hair behind her ears exposing her cherubic face. "How's your morning going?"

I flashed her my *please save me* grin.

"Remember, we are spreading magic," Abby constantly reminded me. "Each time we ship a wand out, we send our blessings as well. They always come back to us three-fold."

This was her business philosophy being an established successful artist, jeweler, and writer in the pagan community who started a goddess movement. She'd created a spiral goddess collection in Northern California. Some of her pieces are permanently displayed in the Smithsonian Museum as part of their Women history collection. Abby was also a staunch advocate in the feminist and LGBTQ communities.

We have come a long way from me managing her businesses where we produced magnificent magic wands made of pewter, decked with semi-precious stones, goddess silver jewelry, sculptures, and universal themed prayer books to working together now.

I squeezed her arm. "You're right. I needed to hear that."

"Blessed be."

Every time a Harry Potter movie was released, our sales would soar above the ceiling as our revenue sources were derived from serious practicing Wiccans, new-age metaphysical outlets, as well as parents of children following Harry Potter.

I remember one slow afternoon, when we bought Starbucks sweets and goodies, settled in the office, stuffed wands in their tubes, inserted spell booklets, and sent off blessings while listening to an audiobook of Joseph Campbell series or Cher ballads on tape.

"I am bipolar," Abby blurted out. "I don't take any medicine for it."

"Oh," I said, not knowing how to react. *No wonder.*

I never knew what her mood would be every time I came to work. She could be the sweetest most loving generous person, but at other times, she acted like a strident petulant child. I loved and accepted both personalities unconditionally.

"On a more serious note, do you have time to come to the warehouse?" Abby asked. "It's the season and I am overwhelmed."

"Yes, dear," I said. "When do you need me?"

"Yesterday!" She grinned.

I had a busy schedule, but when Abby needed me, I always came running. *What are friends for?*

Tension filled the air, while I took a sip of my Cappuccino, then spat it out. "Damn." *What was I thinking when I poured that boiling water?*

Abby nudged me. "Are you okay?"

I bit my lip as her eyes swept my desk. Clearing her throat, she said, "The UPS truck is coming in two hours. We need to get this out today!"

A knot formed in my stomach forcing me to speak faster than usual. "Yes, yes, yes."

Her smile disappeared and transformed into a frown. "And please answer the phone."

The last call I received was from an innocent child, "Will the wands help me clean my room?"

Ring…ring…ring. *One more ring and I'll scream.*

Not paying attention to the caller ID, I rubbed my eyes and picked up the call. "This is Mita, how can I help you?"

A breathy hello filled the air. "Mita, it's Jake," he paused then continued. "I'm afraid I have bad news."

An icy sweat trickled down my nape. A vision of Dad flashed before me then vanished in a second. "Oh no, Dad?"

"He's gone," his voice quivered. "Just a few minutes ago."

"Huh, what do you mean?"

"Dad passed away."

A big blow struck my body while my innards turned into jelly. "No, no, no…he said he'd wait for me!" I raised my voice in denial. "We were still going to Comey Island. I already have my airline ticket for Cebu. This can't be happening."

"Funeral will be in the next few days," Jake asked. "Come home now …"

I hung up before he could finish the sentence.

Glancing at the window, I affixed my gaze at the red oak tree finding comfort in the wind blowing the leaves. It's every child's worst nightmare to learn that their parent has passed away. I don't know if it meant the silver cord was finally cut? Now, that my father was gone, I questioned my mortality. *Why didn't you wait for me to come home Dad?*

Abby stood there with raised eyebrows. At seventy years old, her hearing may have faded, but her perception had heightened with age.

"My father just passed away," I welled up.

Abby straightened her shoulders and heaved a long breath. "I am so sorry, Mita." She reached out to me and gave me a tight embrace. The world spun and my heart raced. Like on cue, Abby held me closer allowing me to focus on the rise and fall of her breathing. She gripped me tightly and said, "You can do this. Don't worry about work. You need to get on that plane now."

After bidding Abby goodbye, I eyed the stack of folders and brushed my thoughts aside. Work can wait . . . I strode toward my car, opened the door, and slid into the driver's seat. Upon starting the ignition, I spotted a golden monarch hovering around. It flapped its beautiful yellow wings while circling me.

I blinked. *Dad?*

Is this another sign? Yellow is Dad's favorite color which signifies hope. Dad had always had a positive outlook in life and this trait help him overcome the numerous battles he's faced in his life.

Before releasing the break and closing the door, the monarch fluttered in. *Is this really you, Dad?*

I turned the radio on and while bracing myself for a good forty-five-minute drive home from Benicia to Moraga. The music caught my attention. *Dad, this is your favorite song.*

And now, the end is near, so I'll face the final curtain... I turned off the ignition.

Drying my tears, I sang at the top of my lungs, "My Way," by Frank Sinatra. Dad's national anthem.

"For what is a man, what has he got,

If not himself then he has not

To say all the things, he truly feels

And not the words of one who kneels.

The record shows, I took the blows,

But I did it my way."

Dad sang this song at every party or Karaoke opportunity and this moment felt so surreal like he was crooning to me. Moments later, a strong familiar scent pervaded the car, Dad's favorite cologne, Old Spice aftershave. *I miss you, Dad. Why did you have to die without saying goodbye to me?*

Taking the next exit, I whispered a solemn prayer aloud, "May you rest in peace, Dad. I'm sorry I wasn't there on time."

A vision of him flashed through my mind. He was young once again, dashing with a twinkle in his eyes and no trace of lines and weariness in his face, "I'll be home soon, Dad. I love you."

4 THE WAKE

November 2010

Battered from the long stretch of an eighteen-hour flight from San Francisco, I arrived in Cebu at dusk with my younger sister, Candy. She stepped out of the airplane fresh as a rose, wearing a tracksuit which complimented her round, symmetrical face and beautiful doe eyes, while I looked beat-up and worn out in my pair of jeans and a loose sweater. We were complete opposites, me as the quiet introspective older sister, while she babbled like sweet champagne. But no champagne for us today; our throats were parched, and we longed for water. As we headed toward immigration, we spotted a water fountain and sprinted like we found an oasis in the desert. The liquid quenched our thirst.

She flashed me a weak tired smile. "Are we home yet?"

"We need to get our luggage."

The enduring moment gave us time to tame our wild emotions, process Dad's passing, and what it could mean for our future?

Candy trailed behind me while I pushed the cart toward the exit. Heat permeated my skin reminding me that we were in the tropics, and I didn't need my sweater.

"I don't remember Cebu being this humid." Candy wiped her neck.

I grinned.

We hailed a taxi and didn't say a word until we arrived home. Upon reaching the premises, the entire neighborhood was dark except for the dim streetlights. An array of cars was parked outside the driveway, and there was a faint sound of people chanting the rosary inside.

Candy and I stepped out of the cab and approached the garage.

Tall, withered weeds surrounded us.

Candy covered her mouth. "What on earth happened here?"

I shrugged. "They must be grieving for Dad too."

My legs wobbled as we entered through the sliding glass doors of our ancestral home. I scanned the foyer, noting that it was exactly how Mom left it years ago with her grand dilapidated piano displayed on the right side. Running my fingers on the fine glazed wood, I stood still. Mom would have disapproved seeing how the polish had chipped away from neglect and abandonment.

Candy nudged me from behind as we crossed through the dining hall. "Look at those leaks and stains above."

I followed her gaze. "What a waste." This dining hall hosted a generation of family occasions and seeing how Mom had kept all our family pictures warmed my heart. Our antique *'Narra', a* hand-carved dining table, was shoved into a corner to make way for Dad's coffin.

Candy grasped my hand as we watched the chairs filled with people extending to the patio. Friends, relatives, and strangers came out of the woodworks to pay homage and their last respects to Dad. While I recognized some of them, other faces seemed unfamiliar to me.

A lump formed in my throat, recalling how we used to run back and forth as kids welcoming constant visitors with a wide smile. *But not today, today is a day of mourning, a day of sorrow, a day I will never forget.*

Dad laid peacefully with flowers, cards, and gifts were strewn around his coffin.

"Dad." I burst into tears while Candy rubbed my back and wept. If only I could touch his face once more for the very last time. I wanted to hug him so tight and express all the feelings that were bursting out of me but seeing him so fragile hindered me. I was fearful his body would disintegrate and turn into ashes.

"Dad, you said you were going to wait for me. We were going to Comey Island, remember?"

They extended Dad's wake to give our family a chance to fly from all over the world to come home and pay our last respects. Signs of fungi emerged from his skin. It was time to bury Dad. But was I ready to bury my emotions and feelings, along with all these things we should have said to one another, words left unspoken?

Dad had physical frailties as old age caught up with him.

A stroke caused paralysis on the left half of his body, and he could barely walk. "You can rest now, Dad."

"Yes, Dad. You are in a better place." Candy chimed in before excusing herself to greet the guests.

Dad was a recluse in his remaining days who rarely came out of his room, but despite that, the number of people that showed up today was an indication that he'd touched many lives.

Tito Ralph, my dad's youngest brother who could pass for an Italian man with his bronze skin and aristocratic nose inched his way forward to the coffin. His deep-set eyes pierced through me while he wept in deep prayer. "*Manoy* is gone." His eyes welled up.

My heart broke and all I could say was, "Tito, I am so glad you are here. This means a lot to my family. Thank you, *Tito*." Dad's bloodline was enmeshed with his through a mutual mother, but they had different fathers. My grandmother was a young widow when my paternal grandfather died, and she remarried. Dad's relationship with his youngest brother was temperamental. It was hot, cold, loving, spiteful and the last couple of years they had not exchanged a word to one another. But to my surprise, I learned that *Tito* Ralph had been at the wake daily since Dad's passing. The pain, love, and remorse were etched all over his grim face.

As soon as she saw me, Dahlia, my dad's live-in companion excused herself from the elderly ladies who hovered around her and approached me. Her long, straight hair which she often let loose was now tied in a bun exposing her sunken cheeks, dark circles, and gaunt face. She was chubbier the last time I saw her a couple of years ago. We hugged, streaming in tears and for a moment I had forgotten that she was only in her thirties.

"He had a stroke again." She dried her eyes. "I slapped his face hoping he would regain consciousness, but he didn't wake up," she relayed all the details of his last few breaths on earth before collapsing in her arms. "I tried to revive him, but it was too late."

It was not Dad's first stroke and most likely his third stroke which compelled the nurses to teach Dahlia what to do in case it would happen again.

More and more, guests arrived and expressed their heartfelt condolences. Barely having any sleep from the flight back home, all I wanted to do was close my eyes and rest in a soft, comfortable bed, but instead, I continued to greet the visitors and thanked them for coming over.

A little fair-skinned eight-year-old boy with jet-black curly locks and deep-set eyes ran toward Dahlia.

"Macky?" I bent down and squeezed his cheek.

Macky brought my hand to his forehead, a sign of greeting and respect for elders to request their blessing which is known to be a Filipino custom similar to kissing on the cheek. *"Mano Ate."*

His Caucasian features made us suspicious about his lineage and sparked questions regarding his DNA as to whether he was our real brother or half-brother. However, he was born into the family and Dad loved and claimed him as his son. In his golden years, Dad spent more time with him than me or any of my siblings, a harsh reality we all had to swallow.

"You're so grown up and handsome." I pointed to his chest.

He gave me a sheepish grin, while Dahlia beamed with pride.

Facing Dahlia, I said. "I wish we'd met under better circumstances, but I want to thank you for taking care of my father."

I rose from the ground, and we hugged tight.

Swept with a mixture of emotions, my stomach rumbled. I excused myself and headed to the kitchen where the smell of fried food, *Lumpia,* as well as a, marinate of garlic, vinegar, and soy sauce, *Adobo*, haunted me.

I spotted my tall and slender brother Jake with salt and pepper hair and thick glasses. He was munching on *puto* with yellow mango and sipping native *chokolate.* I tapped his shoulder.

Startled, he opened his eyes wide when he saw me. "*Oi,* Mita. When did you arrive?"

I poked his ribs. "You're always eating. I arrived ten, maybe fifteen minutes ago."

We laughed and embraced.

"Have you eaten?" He popped a slice of mango inside his mouth.

"Yes, I mean, no. If you consider airplane food, real food? I am famished." I said, picking up a plate and helping myself to a crispy *Lumpia.*

"There's so much food. You know how wakes are, people seem to care more about the food than the person died," he quipped.

I smiled, savoring the *adobo* and adding more rice to my plate. *Gosh, how I missed home cooking.*

"We will have a meeting later tonight." He said. "By the way, where's Candy?" Jake asked.

"She was entertaining the guests when I left." I wiped my mouth with a napkin. "I'm looking forward to seeing everyone tonight."

***

After all the guests left, Candy and I took a nap and woke up refreshed. All my siblings were finally home. Ironically, people live such busy lives, but when a loved one dies, everybody drops what they are doing to pay their last respect. My family is all spread out living in different countries and it's sad that we only get together for an occasion like this. I understand now, why Dad called all of us to come home in 2008. He wanted to celebrate his life when he was still physically and mentally fit to participate.

That was a wise move, Dad.

My siblings and I gathered in our parent's room. After a brief greet and meet, catching up with each other's lives, we settled right into business as a team and dealt with the logistics of the funeral for the next day. Setting our emotions aside, we all agreed that the how, when, where, and whys had to be addressed accordingly.

"I have a plot at 'Golden Haven' in Consolacion," Manuel, our second eldest brother who just arrived from Seattle with his wife said. He was attractive in a quiet and mysterious way with his fair skin and prominent cheekbones.

"That's awesome, Manuel," Armando, our eldest brother said. Armando had flown in from Cambodia where he was currently residing. Armando had thick jet-black hair, olive-toned skin, and was six-feet tall which was unique for a Filipino man. He emanated strength in his bearing, being the eldest. He was a professional organizer for labor unions and stepped up to arrange the logistics of Dad's funeral as well.

"Mita, you're the historian of the family. Do you want to open the church service and share information about Dad and our family history? After all, you are writing a book about him, right?" Manuel asked.

"Sure." I said, too exhausted to refuse. Everyone was aware, that I was working on a book about Dad. It was our project and he fed me fodder when he was still alive.

"Everyone who wants to say a word or two about Dad can simply speak up," Jake said.

"Let's toast to Dad's life," Rudy, our fourth brother who had a stocky frame, tanned skin, and soft curly locks flashed his enchanting smile exposing his dimples. He opened a bottle of Johnnie Walker Black Label and offered tiny shot glasses to everyone. Rudy who charmed everyone he met believed in numbing the pain rather than dealing with it head-on.

We toasted to our father's life, remembering what a fine, honorable, and loving man he was.

"Here's to you, Dad!" I raised my glass in a toast. "Did you know that Dad had a photographic memory? He did not want to admit his failing eyesight, so he memorized the phone numbers in his contact list."

"Dad was amazing," Jake interjected. "He could easily make friends with the governors, mayors, bankers, etc, and could pull strings for favors from them whether he was in the Philippines, Guam, or Borneo. That's a life skill."

"And a ladies' man," Candy added. "While he was at the hospital in Antioch for a week, all he did was crack jokes and charm all the nurses."

"Yes, he was a comedienne, indeed," Paul our tall, fair-skinned youngest brother who wore thick glasses and just wrapped up his doctorate in science chimed in. "He ribald humor and bawdy jokes broke the ice with anyone he met."

We cheered on Dad's life and celebrated his good qualities until the liquor forced everyone to say goodbye and call it a night.

Moments later, in my old bedroom, I closed my eyes processing everything that transpired from when I'd received the phone call about Dad's passing. The walls seemed to suck the air out of me. As much as Mom was the life force in this house, Dad's energy permeated the air like he was still guarding his fortress. *You may be gone, Dad, but your presence is still here.*

5 THE BURIAL

November 2010

From the corner of my eye, I caught a glimpse of the immaculate sun, yet I chose to keep my sunglasses glued to my face. Tears trickled down my cheeks as family and friends gathered at the 'Golden Haven Memorial Park' at the sprawling hills of Consolacion, Cebu, to bid our final goodbye to our father, Mateo Zara.

There were so many familiar and unfamiliar faces and people were praying or talking about how much they adored him and how he had changed their lives. Even the people from his church loved him. Dad was never religious, but in his last few years, he metamorphosed into a devout, dedicated Christian. I caught him frequently kneeling in prayer and reading his Bible diligently.

Some of Dad's friends went out of their way to commemorate him.

"I became a Christian, because of your dad's influence," Chris introduced himself to me.

"I was baptized at your pool." Diana smiled.

"I have great memories of being in your home, we held our Bible study every week in the living room," another church member relayed to me.

"Your Dad was a loving man," Pastor Roy said. "He was incredibly supportive of our church. We will deeply miss him."

We thanked them for their kind words.

A batch of people in uniform— veterans were present during that day.

Dad was also a veteran, and this reminded me of our Philippine history. On December 8, 1941, the Japanese attacked the Americans in the Philippines. At that time, the Philippines was under the American Commonwealth since the purchase of the Philippines from the 1898 Spanish-American War. The attack drew the Americans into World War II and after that, the Japanese sustained their attacks on the Americans who were on Philippine soil.

President Roosevelt vowed, "So long as the flag of the United States flies on Filipino soil, as a pledge of our duty to your people, it will be defended by our own men to the death."

As citizens of an American commonwealth, Filipino soldiers were legally American nationals, and Roosevelt promised them the same veterans' benefits given to members of the U.S. Armed Forces. Although the latter agreement was controversial, but that's another story to tell.

Under the command of General Douglas MacArthur, Filipinos fought alongside American soldiers against the Japanese. And when the Allied Forces were defeated, McArthur fled to Australia with a famous promise, "I shall return."

Even after the surrender of the Philippines to the Japanese in May of 1942, Filipino guerrilla forces continued to fight the Japanese in the jungles and mountains. Dad was barely a teenager at that time when he enlisted as a guerilla.

"We had to run to the mountains and hide," I recall Dad telling us. "If not, we were all going to be killed."

For three years they kept up their resistance until MacArthur returned with troops that eventually drove out the Japanese. By the time the war ended in 1945, it had claimed a terrible toll, including the deaths of an estimated one million Filipinos.

"When we returned to the city, everything burnt into ashes," Dad had said. "There was nothing left. When school resumed, I took advantage of the situation and accelerated myself to a level higher. After all, there were no records to disprove my case."

This was typical of Dad to seize an opportunity in every disaster.

Through the veterans, Dad obtained a scholarship to pursue a college degree. In his later years, he became a beneficiary of the Veteran's Act and after a long year of arbitration, Dad received a lump sum of cash and a humble pension that supported him until he died. Upon his death, the veterans actively took the reins and honored him with a Veteran's Burial ceremony for his service.

And then, there were the Masons.

"I can go all over the world, and as a Mason, people will help me and accept me as a brother," he had once said. He was proud to be a Mason.

I suspected that was also part of Dad's business success. He knew when to call on a brother for help. For many years, he wore a simple gold band with the Masonic insignia. He used to wear his ring more proudly than his wedding ring. I don't recall him even wearing his wedding ring.

A Mason in his chapter also attended the burial and performed a Masonic funeral rite to honor him as one of their fellows. His Masonic family kept their tradition by visiting us every Christmas to bring good tidings and special holidays food supplies, in the succeeding the years after his death.

Upon laying down his coffin in the ground, we threw flowers into his grave. Who is Mateo Zara? Was he a father, an engineer, a politician, a businessman, a mason, a veteran, a guerilla, a born-again Christian, a lost abandoned child or the adulterer? *Whoever he was, Dad was the best father a daughter could ever have.*

Just when Dad was laid to rest in eternity, whispers amongst the crowd erupted. "Psst, Vera is here!"

Gazing at the crowd, I spotted a petite lady garbed in black and bowed down in prayer. Vera was Dad's Executive Secretary for many years since the Seventies. When Dad was released from prison in 1977, he had opened a company in Manila where she had risen from being a secretary to becoming the Vice President of the company.

What the heck is she doing here, crocodile tears? Cray-cray!

Seeing Vera again triggered a memory of when my mom had returned to Cebu to claim back her life and the lifestyle she was accustomed to, I was living in Manila working for Dad's company at that time. He had always let Vera accompany me to shop and travel during those opportunities.

If I needed to go clothes shopping, Dad had suggested. "Vera is the best shopping buddy."

On my eighteenth birthday, my first trip out of the country, Dad 'gifted me' a trip to Hong Kong, but Vera was my constant chaperone. I seemed to have spent more time with Vera than with Dad.

When we had our outings, Vera used to say, "You are your dad's favorite daughter." And then, she had added, "Don't you ever grow fat!" The latter sentence stuck in my brain and I can't comprehend 'til this day why she had given me that painful remark. *What did she mean by that?*

Many years later when I fled the country and lived in Germany in the Eighties, Mom and my sister, Candy visited me and that is when I discovered the real story between Dad and Vera. She was indeed his mistress!

Heaving a sigh, I recalled the last time I went out with Vera many years ago as we celebrated her husband Tom's birthday. Vera, Tom, Dad, and I painted the town red with dinner and dancing. I may have been so naive then, but I still cannot fathom why they had such an arrangement?

When Dad won a bid to work in Brunei in the Eighties, Mom was excited to relocate to Brunei and start a new life with Dad. Unfortunately, Vera was already settled in there with Dad. Mom was crushed, humiliated, and heartbroken when she discovered their affair and realized that Dad had no intentions of taking her all along. She packed her bags, sold everything she possessed, left Cebu after she'd paid all of Dad's debt, and came visited me in Germany before she and my sister Candy relocated to America.

Standing a foot away from Vera, something nudged me that today was a day of reckoning. I had been fantasizing for a long time, that when I'd see her, I would clobber and beat her up for that ultimate betrayal. *Why did she have to come here?* All I wanted to do was yank her hair, slap her face, and spit at her for all that she did to my family. *This one's for you, Mom!*

But when our eyes met, I maintained my composure and flashed her a solemn smile.

She was no longer the home wrecker sex goddess who had fair skin, a small waist, and curvy hips, but now a pathetic, older, bloated woman with puffed-up cheeks and uneven patches of her skin. I did not know if I should resent her or feel sorry for her. The voice of reason prevailed! *When they go low, you go high. The universe will take care of itself. Justice will always prevail and Karma's a bitch!*

Looking up to the sky, I made a mental note. *Not today, this is dad's day, a day to honor his life.*

The song "My Way" played from the background then slowly faded like a distant memory.

6 BAD DREAM

November 2010

Exhausted from attending Dad's funeral, I sought solace in a corner at home and plopped into a couch. I raised my legs to my chest in a fetal position hoping to sleep and escape into another world. My tank was empty from processing the day's event which entailed an early mass in the church, then a thirty-minute drive to the cemetery, mingling with all the well-wishers, followed by an emotional crying fit, feeding the crowd, opening the envelopes and cards, dealing with family, the helpers, while jetlagged and caught between two time zones. Being drowsy and cranky did not help in confronting the past, present, and future. The task was enormous, and the weight was too much to carry. A part of me was fading away.

Jake spotted me curled up in a bun. Sensing my need to rest, he offered, "You can stay in Dad's room."

"Thank you." I rose from the couch and headed toward the hallway.

Upon stepping inside Dad's room, I scanned the surroundings noticing his bed was moved to its original position at the center of the room. The last time I was in Cebu, I remember Dad's bed had shifted from one corner of the room next to the window, where he could watch people playing tennis in the court across from his room. He had a cozy nook with an aged worn-out sofa, so he could catch up with his news and spend time watching satellite movies or *Tagalog* flicks. Dad's energy emanated from the walls to the table where he read his Bible, wrote in his journal, and in his last years, ate his meals.

Sadness loomed over me as I smelled his pillow and stroked the sheets. There were faint traces of his Old Spice cologne. A deep sense of regret washed upon me for not visiting him as much as I should have. *Dang! What kind of a daughter was I?*

Before hitting the sack, I sent a quick prayer and shot a warning, "Don't you dare show up, Dad. I get scared easily!" A deep slumber enveloped me.

Moments later, an urge to pee woke me up from my sleep. Checking the clock, I noted it was midnight. After relieving my bladder, I sprung to the bed hoping to get forty winks. A transparent fog-like presence settled in Dad's favorite chair next to the bed. I bolted upright. Am I dreaming? A loud thud rocked my chest, while a cold wave sent shivers from my neck down to my spine.

"Dad, is this you?" I squinted my eyes to get a clearer vision.

The presence formed into an image. I inched forward to get a closer look at a young man wearing trousers. No more wrinkles, gray hair, and pale skin. Blinking twice, I realized it was Dad—a younger and healthier version of him.

He flashed me a sweet smile while his eyes twinkled. "Don't be sad, I'm in a good place right now and with your mom. Everything that had happened was meant to be. So please, don't worry my darling."

Tears trickled down my cheek. I hugged my knees with my arms in a curled position.

"Dad, why did you leave me again? I have always needed you. You said you would wait for me, and we were going to Comey Island. Why didn't you wait for me, Dad?"

He caressed my cheek.

I closed my eyes, cherishing the moment. "You were always gone, Dad. All my life, you were coming and going. I need you now more than ever."

All the pent-up emotions from my childhood raged inside me.

"I am here now and will always be with you forever. I promise you that," He whispered, slowly fading away, while I was left alone again to collect my thoughts.

I opened my eyes as his scent continued to pervade the room. I reached out my hands, hoping to pull him back, but a white smoke sizzled and left without a trace of his existence.

A warm sensation showered upon me knowing from the depth of my soul that he is watching over me as promised. I'm glad I had made my peace. My fears dissipated into thin air as I closed my eyes again. At the depths of my sleep, I was transported into another space and time.

The memory dam broke, and all the scenes from the past I chose to bury resurfaced.

***

December 1972

I was 12 again.

Early December nights always brought good tidings during the holiday season, and everyone was in a benevolent and generous mood. Our tradition involved welcoming a group of carolers, who sang us a litany of Christmas songs.

I was a happy-go-lucky child who cherished Christmas and had a good appetite. An aroma of garlic and coconut vinegar, *suka* from the *adobo*, and the *mungo* soup lingered from our kitchen. I could not resist dipping my finger in the *adobo* sauce and tasting it, "Yum!"

"When can we eat?" I asked, heading toward the dining room to join Mom and Candy at the dinner table.

Mom looked glamorous with her coiffed beehive hairdo, wearing a loose and colorful traditional *batik* caftan. I always adored her fair porcelain smooth complexion, dark ebony hair, almond eyes with thick lashes. Her best asset was her smile. She smiled on all occasions whether she was happy or sad and sat at our table poised like a beauty queen. "Patience my dear."

I forced a smile wishing it were as pretty as hers. "What time is Dad coming home?"

"Soon." Mom said.

My brother Paul played ball in the front yard with my cousin Ray while we waited for the meal to be served.

I'm hungry.

"Paul, dinner is almost ready." Mom called out to him.

"I'm almost done." Paul hollered back.

Candy glared at me as I tinkered with the fork and spoon while drumming the plate and glass.

I ignored her and continued producing annoying sounds. With my four older brothers living outside of our island, I was stuck with Candy and Paul.

Paul joined us at the table with a wide beam.

"Did you wash your hands, Paul?" Mom asked.

Paul nodded. "I have a joke. Knock, knock, who's there?" He sat down beside me.

"Tennis," Candy replied. "Tennis who?"

"Tennis is five plus five!"

"Okay, another one…" Candy faced me. "Your turn."

"No, I can't." A queasy knot formed in my tummy.

"Why not?" Candy prodded.

I chewed on the *adobo* which now tasted bland. Tightness gripped my chest triggering nausea.

"Mita, are you okay?" Mom touched my forehead.

Heart racing, I couldn't comprehend why I was feeling this way. Before I could respond to Mom, incessant barking intruded the Christmas songs playing from the background radio.

Loud voices erupted from the shadows while our maid rushed to the front door.

This evening would prove foreboding and the events of this night would resonate in my memory for the years to come. Even as I write this many decades later, the wounds are still fresh. I continue to tremble; confusion and fear haunts me until today. It was the Christmas season that would change my family's lives forever.

Mom rose from her seat to check out the commotion. A look of dread crossed her pretty face, as she watched the men saunter toward our living room.

I swallowed hard. Despite their bulging bellies, their guns were visible in their holsters. They informed my mother that they were from the National Bureau of Investigations (NBI)

Men in civilian and military uniform stepped inside our home. "*Maayo*, is anyone home?"

Among them was a familiar face; Tito Barry the Chief of the NBI folded his arms. His receding hairline and glasses did not overshadow his dignified stance and demeanor. "Good evening, Heike, is Mateo around?"

I recognized Tito Barry as Dad's golf and mahjong buddy. He was not my biological uncle, but he was a close family friend. But this time, he looked and acted like a different person in his professional uniform—a stricter version compared to the jovial, warm, witty person I knew.

Mom stroked her hair, perhaps looking for some way to warn Dad before he arrived home. "He's playing golf. Is there something you need from him that way I can inform him that you are here?" she asked.

Appearing to have sensed Mom's discomfort, Tito Barry answered her, "Mateo is invited to speak with the Provincial Commander of Cebu."

Candy, Paul, and I stood there watching the other men from a corner. *Something wasn't right.*

With crossed eyebrows, Mom contorted into a frown. She informed us before about rumors of these *invitations*, which was a form of deception because some families had never heard from their loved ones again!

"Mateo should be home soon. Coffee or anything to drink?" She paced around the room and appeared like she was trying to mask her fears.

"Coffee please." Tito Barry and his entourage settled into the living room couch.

Mom requested that the maid bring snacks as well.

Nobody said a word while the coffee and freshly baked, butter-rich *ensaymayda* were served. Mom's fingers trembled as she attempted to make small talk while the officers helped themselves to the sumptuous snacks.

"You have a really beautiful house. How long have you lived here, Ma'am?" One officer asked.

"We moved here in 1965," Mom said while glancing around like she was anticipating Dad's arrival any moment.

There was more idle chat, but no one talked about the elephant in our living room. An uncomfortable hour passed before Dad returned home from our local country club, Club Filipino. He frequented the golf course as if it was his day job. I thought he worked there because he usually played a round of golf before he went to work. Dad was a civil engineer and operated a construction company in Cebu that had several operating branches on the surrounding islands. He considered the golf course his social business park.

"Million pesos deals are sealed on a round of golf," Dad had said and encouraged us to play golf as soon as we could grip a club. Golf was a family affair. After church on Sundays, our family frequently played golf. Mom loved hiking the course. She also enjoyed shopping for ladies' golf accessories from golf 'skirts' to designer clubs, shoes, gloves, and accessories. She always provided matching sets of outfits for my sister and me. We were a fashionable tribe back then, trekking the golf course without a care in the world.

Finally, the car screeched into the driveway, Tito Barry rose from his seat and approached the glass door extending to the patio to meet Dad. The rest of the officers stood up and trailed behind him.

Carrying his golf sports bag, Dad strode inside and greeted Tito Barry with a bear hug. "Hey, what brings you here, *Bai*?" Dad stood just five feet four inches tall with a slender built wearing a sporty mustard jersey shirt and slacks. I watched him glowing in his bronze skin as he smiled with his playful eyes. The smell of his Old Spice cologne lingered in the room.

"Mat, you are officially invited by the Provincial Commander of Cebu for interrogations," he said.

Dad muttered, *"Pesteng yawah,"* under his breath.

My siblings and I did not leave the living room, and from the corner of my eye, I witnessed Candy biting her nails while Paul cracked his knuckles.

Earlier this year on September 21, 1972, President Ferdinand Marcos declared Martial Law. I did not know what it meant. People worried about how it would affect their daily lives. A curfew was instated. Only one newspaper and one TV station was allowed to operate, and propaganda was set up to instill fear in every Filipino household. We heard about a lot of arrests going on, student activists, NPA's, and politicians from the opposite parties. People were scrutinizing my family and anticipating Dad's arrest too, especially because he was a politician from the opposite party. My family was fully aware that this could happen any moment, yet we never anticipated it would be today,

With a solemn look on Tito Barry's face, he addressed Dad. "I am sorry Mat, but we need to search your house."

"Uhm, why?" Dad hesitated.

Before Tito Barry could respond, Dad must have realized it was futile to argue with an officer, so he dared Tito Barry to take him with him. "Go ahead."

The officers scattered throughout our home, down the hallways, inside our bedrooms, and into our private lives. Tito Barry sipped his coffee with Dad like it was an ordinary day, discussing the golf game and scores.

Loud voices exploded from our parents' bedroom. The men brought out his collection of firearms and revolvers: Smith and Wesson, Colts, Browning, Ruger, and H&K's, which were hidden in one of the closets. He had enough to supply a private army.

The blood drained from Dad's face as if he had seen a ghost.

Candy, Paul, and I held hands while my mother maintained her composure. I wanted to tell these men to leave our house, but I also wondered why Dad needed to have all these weapons?

"What did you expect me to do? I need to protect myself." Dad reasoned that other member of his family had already been targeted and killed because of their political activities, and he had also been threatened. But the NBI had what they came for which was to arrest my dad by ASSO, an Arrest and Seizure Order.

I later learned the details of events and the relationships that led up to my family's tragedy—a tale of political and social intrigue that set the scene for my father becoming a target of the Marcos regime. By the time the NBI arrived at our door, my father had lost a brother to an assassination that many people suspected had been meant for him. We discovered that much of Dad's family had been targeted. Romeo Borello was a brilliant, promising young lawyer who had helped my dad in his bid for Congress. Romeo also happened to be his half-brother as his father died early and his mother remarried. Romeo was married to Suzette, known to me as Tita Suzy.

The murder took place the night they had taken a client to an invitation-only dinner, the soft opening of a new local restaurant owned by a distant relative.

Tito Romeo had informed my family that around Six PM, three uninvited guests appeared, and Tito Romeo recognized one as a relative from a branch of the extended family but was nonetheless wary of him. Shaking the man's hand, Tito Romeo reportedly laughed and said, "I heard that you were hired to go after me." The man smiled back and assured Romeo his information was wrong. Sensing foul play, Tito Romeo told his wife to go back to the kitchen for her safety. Tita Suzy was adamant to stay and not leave his side while dinner was served perhaps to seal the peace. Tito Romeo paid the bill for both tables. His relative rose and walked over to Tito Romeo who stood to accept his handshake.

But rather than a gesture of gratitude, the handshake was a signal for his two companions who marched to the table, pulled their guns and shot Tito Romeo three times point blank with a .46 caliber pistol. Romeo fell to the ground. One of the companions, a notorious police character, pumped three additional bullets into his prostrate body making sure Romeo was dead. Tito Romeo died after being struck with six deadly bullets.

Dad was on the neighboring island of Davao when he received the tragic news about his brother.

He immediately took the first flight to Cebu. At the funeral, he did his best to console and comfort my aunt, Tita Suzy, promising her that for the rest of his life he'd protect she and her family. Inconsolable, Tita Suzy was reeling with anger and cried out, "Where were you, can you bring him back to life?"

True to his word, Dad took personal responsibility for Tito Romeo's death and his family. He provided for their subsistence until they were mature and independent adults.

Tito Axel, my other uncle, had himself narrowly escaped death. He was the mayor of Comey Island, as well as being a medical doctor. Shortly after the last election in 1965, Axel was ambushed while walking down a quiet road in his town and left for dead. Thanks to an alert bodyguard who sensed trouble and shouted a warning, Axel ducked, and the assassin's bullet missed its deadly mark. The bullet shattered Tito Axel's leg and left him disabled for life. Even though he was shot forcing him to walk with a cane, Tito Axel carried on with town business.

Later, fourteen political leaders under him were kidnapped and brought to Davos city. While six of them managed to escape, there was no trace as to what happened to the eight politicians. Among those who had escaped was Allan. He was crucified and tortured but lived to tell the tale.

Two weeks later, the son of Congressman Raymond Davide and his henchmen came to Comey Island, looking for my Tito Axel. When they could not find him, they riddled his house with bullets as well as shooting the neighboring houses at the *población*. Finally, his home was bombed. Congressman Raymond Davide was rumored to be a warlord in the district. Davide owned vast portions of land, sugar plantations, cement factories, and manufactured his arsenal of weapons. At the same time, Davide also developed infrastructures such as roads, bridges, and schools for the benefit of his town. He was feared and loved at the same time; Davide had a reputation for eliminating his political enemies and people who got in the way of his ambitions.

Tito Axel secretly fled to Cebu with his family, seeking temporary sanctuary with us and with other relatives. They later, migrated to the United States, there he sought asylum, abandoning politics altogether pursuing a successful career in the medical field.

This was the political climate in the Philippines during the Marcos regime. In the 1960s, widespread corruption existed, polls were bought, ballots rigged, and voters were threatened and suppressed at gunpoint. It was with this backdrop that Dad decided to run for Congress in 1965 and again in 1969 against incumbent Congressman Raymond Davide.

After the assassination of Tito Romeo, and the attempt on the life of Tito Axel, Mama Lingling my grandmother, who was a renowned matriarch and socialite, became a voice in this struggle.

"Justice for my sons," she'd plead with the public. The culmination of the assassination and attempted shootings of our family members was big news and had scored her the cover of *The Free Press*, a political magazine. Every line on her pained face was etched on the cover. Her mascara-smeared eyes, drenched in tears screamed for justice.

After all that had transpired, Dad never again left the house without wearing his heavy bulletproof vest. Everywhere he went bodyguards routinely escorted him, he was conscious that anytime it could be his turn.

On the day of my father's arrest, as Tito Barry exposed the extent of my father's arsenal, my mom's strength waned and exposed her pale cheeks. I still believe she had not been aware that firearms were stashed in a corner of her walk-in dressing room.

Dad headed to his bedroom while Mom ambled behind him with shoulders slumped.

Candy, Paul, and I exchanged glances then I dashed to my bedroom as tears lagged down my cheeks. I picked up Nancy, my talking doll, and held her close to my chest and then went to my parent's bedroom.

The door was left ajar, so I witnessed everything.

"Mat, what is this all about?" Mom asked.

"Nothing." Dad shrugged like he was expecting Mom to understand the depth of his silence more than his words.

Trembling, Mom packed his clothes in a small Samsonite suitcase as if Dad was leaving for just another business trip.

"How many days will you be gone?" She asked.

But Dad just stared at her with blank eyes.

Night had fallen and the blazing equatorial moon illuminated the front of the house like the sun, exposing everything that was happening inside. Dad walked to the military car parked outside our house while the neighbors watched and whispered.

Peering through my bedroom window, I held my breath clinging to Nancy. With tiny hands, I opened the window hoping to tell him that I love him but could only catch a glimpse of his silhouette. "Bye, Dad." I whispered.

He bowed his head and the car sped away, while my heart deflated like a balloon.

7 GASPING FOR AIR

December 1972

A feeling of emptiness and dread lingered in the dining room and enveloped me. Twenty-four hours had passed since Dad was taken and everything seemed like a blur for me. I gasped for air while Candy and Paul had grim looks marked on their faces. Mom withdrew into silence while dinner was served. Her blank stares offered no words or explanation for what had just happened. Difficult months and years ahead awaited her. A woman raising children on her own in a harsh and forbidding macho culture would raise eyebrows.

Although Mom did not show she was overwhelmed by the situation, she was most likely thankful that my two older brothers were already living abroad. I knew that something was very wrong, and that life would never be the same for me. I did not understand how Tito Barry who was Dad's friend, could do this to him? As a Catholic child, I thought of Judas' betrayal kiss to Jesus.

I broke the silence. "Mom, where are they taking Dad?"

Mom took a sip of water, oblivious to her surroundings. My question was left unanswered. Mom could only stare into the distance, shooting holes into space.

We were mutually bewildered, but I persisted. "When will he come home?"

She looked at me briefly and forced an empty smile.

After dinner, I locked the door inside my bedroom acknowledging that I had not only lost my dad, but I had also lost my mother. She gradually retreated into a private world of her own.

Various newspapers were scattered on my bed. Perusing the pages, the headlines of local and national papers blared, "Conspirators of the Assassination of President Marcos Arrested." To make matters worse, it was also broadcasted throughout all the local radio and television stations that were allowed to operate under the 'New Society'— which was just another name for Martial Law. Dad was one of the many politicians arrested in an alleged conspiracy to assassinate President Marcos.

The news of Dad's arrest punched me right through my gut, although I did not fully understand the depth of the accusation. At my young age, I did not even know what the word *conspiracy* meant. I could not fully grasp the meaning of "Martial Law" either.

A wave of nausea surged through me as I replayed the catastrophe that happened the night before. *How could Tito Barry stab my father in the back?* This was my Tito Barry who joined us for Sunday dinners and shared humorous stories with us. He played poker and golf with Dad and stayed later for drinks. He was a regular presence in our house. I simply could not understand why he'd come to arrest my dad. I was stung with shame as if I carried the sins of my father without even knowing what those sins were.

I longed for the earth to swallow me up, burying me ten feet beneath the rubble, stone and soil. Not knowing what to expect, I tore all the newspapers until they were shredded into small pieces and burst into tears. Clinging to Nancy, I combed her blonde, shaggy uneven hair hoping to make sense of it all.

I pressed the button in the middle of her vinyl body.

Nancy said, "Everything's going to be alright, Mommy!"

I pressed it again.

"I'm hungry, where's my milk? I want to play."

I listened to her repeatedly, noticing that the boring phrases seemed comforting.

Curling myself into fetal position while crying myself to sleep, hoping for the night to envelop my fears I resigned myself to the safety of my dreams. *When will I see you again, Dad?*

8 THE AFTERMATH

November 2010

A few days after the funeral, my siblings had packed their clothes ready to return to their countries and get back to their lives. Yet before leaving, my brothers called for a final meeting.

We gathered inside Dad's bedroom, which was now filled with a stack of boxes.

"Why don't we go through Dad's boxes together, keep what's relevant and throw out what we think is not?" Jake suggested as he handed us one box each.

"Good idea," I said, going through Dad's imprints.

"Dad was really big on journal writing." Candy picked up a notebook and went through its contents.

"I agree." I nodded. "It was easy to buy him gifts for Christmas. He always wanted planners or nice executive logbooks and pens." A painful jab hit me as I recalled sorting out Mom's things when she passed away, realizing that we were doing the same thing for

Dad. "He recorded everything he did in his daily life, unlike Mom who collected prayers."

"What are we going to do about all these correspondences?" Paul asked while sorting out the boxes.

"Just pick what you think is important and throw the rest away." Jake pointed toward a garbage bin.

"And all these files from court cases?" Armando asked, perusing the files.

I glanced at the files. "Maybe, can we dump it in the garbage? There is no use keeping that now. Dad had many pending cases. He was frequently sued for business malpractices, and he always countersued in return."

"In business, you've got to develop thick elephant skin," Dad used to advise me.

Being back at my parent's home sent me back into an avalanche of childhood memories both happy and sad.

I remembered our parents' room had a desk on one sidewall and good lighting so that we could turn on the air condition and created an atmosphere conducive to studying.

"Do you guys recall how we used to sit here in this room and Mom helped us with our homework?" I asked.

"Yeah, I remember. Mom was a good educator," Candy said.

"I hated it," I said. "Every time I asked her something, she never gave me a direct answer. She always said why don't you research it? Moms always had a comeback for my questions."

Mom was a teacher and she had consistently checked our homework, writings, reports, and essays. She had stacked our library with encyclopedias and classical books. Mom raised us to read books and encouraged us do to research. I'm proud to say that my entire family are avid readers.

Taking a break from sorting out Dad's items, I plopped onto their bed, scanning all the corners of the room feeling empty that both my parents were now gone.

Mom had decked their bed with silky satin sheets, and I could still remember how they felt against my skin. At the end of the bed was a beautiful hand-carved exotic oriental wooden trunk where she had kept her linens.

"What happened to Mom's precious trunk?" I asked. Every time she opened the trunk, it smelled of cedar and rosewood. The distinct smell has stayed with me throughout adulthood.

"She must have sold it," Jake said. "She had to raise money to pay off Dad's debts."

"Too bad." I pursed my lips. "I would have wanted to keep it." Every time, I moved into a new house, I tried to recreate Mom's bedroom, looking for similar trunks to remind me of her and of our childhood.

I remember the intricate altar that she had built in the right corner of their room. This was the life force of our family. My mother believed in the saying that, "A family that prays together, stays together." She had a collection of life-size statues of Jesus, the Blessed Virgin Mary, and all the saints adorned with fancy candles and a collection of signature rosaries.

"Do you remember how we used to pray at this corner of the room and do the rosary?" I asked.

"We were no longer home." Jake flashed me a smile.

"Oh, yes I remember." Paul crossed his legs.

"I hated it. I felt we were being punished!" I smirked.

It was not rare to have an altar in every Filipino household. It was also common to have a Catholic grotto in their gardens depending on their financial status. The Filipinos take pride in being the only Christian country in the Far East. But I believe Asians, in general, are accustomed to setting up an altar in their homes, whether they are practicing Buddhism, Hinduism, or Islam.

"Did Mama Lingling take you on her rounds of the church as well?" I asked my siblings. Referring to our grandmother Lingling, who was petite, charming, elegant, and the matriarch powerhouse of the clan. She was also a devoted fervent seeker.

"She tried with no success because Mom always rescued me." Rudy laughed while flipping the pages of Dad's journals.

"I remember visiting eight churches with Mama one Sunday." Paul chimed in.

My grandma, Mama Lingling was a passionate churchgoer, she visited several places of worship to find the right fit. She habitually dressed in a brown garb to represent her affiliation with the Carmelite order as a form of penance and to renounce worldliness.

"I had to kneel and pray with her from the entrance of the Santo Niño Church to the altar like this." Rudy knelt, moved one knee forward, and demonstrated how it was done. "Otherwise, she wouldn't give me an allowance."

I laughed remembering how our grandmother did this regularly when she was paying homage to Santo Niño, the patron saint of Cebu. Occasionally, she would take a reluctant family member with her. It was a blessing to her, but a curse for the selected chosen one.

Mom was overly critical of her mother-in-law, although unconsciously she resembled her ways of visiting the churches. She also explored different sects of Christianity, from Catholicism and Charismatic groups to evangelicals, until she had found what was most comfortable to her. When I was twelve, she was still a practicing Catholic.

Memories of our altar brought me back to the time after Dad had been arrested. We lit candles and prayed daily for a grueling hour or two. I had no choice but to acquiesce to Mom's demands, but I thought I was being persecuted for Dad's detainment.

December 1972

Although that altar no longer exists, still the past beckoned and opened a portal to the aftermath of Dad's arrest. Before going to school Mom would gather us in her room in front of that elaborate homemade altar to join her in her morning prayer session.

"Huhuuuuuu," she would wail, praying for God to bring Dad back home. Once I remember her desperate pleas were interrupted by the sound of the phone ringing. She rose from her knees and answered the call. After she put down the phone, Mom informed us that it was Dad, he explained that it was the first chance he was given to call and asked if we, the children, had heard about what happened to him.

How could anyone not know about it?

After our morning prayers, I kept my head bowed down while dragging my feet to the car. Nothing about this day seemed right. *My life is doomed.*

I looked back at my mom, who was already on the phone again. "Do I really need to go to school today?"

"Absolutely! Hurry now, or you will be late." Mom shooed me away, anxious to get rid of me to return to her phone conversation.

"I need to talk to Dad, Mom. Can you get the phone number of the prison so I can call him when I get back from school?" Stood my ground. "Maybe Tito Barry knows where Dad is?" Persisted. "He arrested him after all, why did he do that Mom?"

"Can you please go now? Have many things to do." Mom raised her voice. "GO!"

"Mom, I feel sick! I have a stomachache," I pleaded.

"No more excuses, you kids will be late. Please go now!" My siblings were already waiting for me in the car with the driver.

I reluctantly stepped inside the car, slumped in the chair, and pulled the car door forcefully with a loud, *bang.* Tears flowed, while I gazed out the window on the way to school.

Moments later, we arrived at St. Theresa's, an exclusive Catholic girls' school run by strict Belgian nuns in Cebu. Attending this school was considered a privilege, but for me it was penance. Hated every day at school. Despite our humid and hot tropical climate, we were made to wear uncomfortable starched and ironed uniforms. Along with that daily discomfort, I had a serious self-image problem that added to my daily dread of school.

I didn't have the white skin that is the treasured sign of beauty in the Philippines; my complexion was dark, and I was self-conscious about my weight thinking I was fat. I was fed on my mother's perspectives of female beauty, and they never seem to match my appearance.

In school, we were also required to speak English and fined for conversing in our local dialect. All that repression created an atmosphere in which vicious bullying among the students was a daily occurrence. Whether in our native tongue of Visayan or in English, I was a favored target. The cruelty escalated after my father was taken away.

Most of my schooling at St. Theresa's was a dull and painful blur. God was the center of the nuns' teachings toward the goal of raising God-fearing, pious, and submissive Catholics.

Math class on Monday mornings was torture and I could hardly concentrate. Once while doing a math exercise in class, my pencil broke, and I realized I'd been holding the pencil so tightly that it snapped. Streaming with rage, I raised my voice. "I can't do this!"

Heads turned toward my direction, followed by footsteps. My math teacher approached me. "You know that yelling is prohibited inside the classroom."

Swallowed hard, and then nodded. "I'm sorry."

With stern eyes, she picked up my pencil.

Dang! Forgot to bring my sharpener.

Whispers filled the air then the bell rang.

Phew...

Just when I thought that I was saved by the bell, we were summoned to do confession which for me was the worst part of my Catholic upbringing.

Carrying my heavy school bag, my classmates and I marched in one fine line toward Redemptorist church that was across the street from the school campus. A pebble caused me to drop my bag and lose my balance. I landed on my knees; blood gushed out.

Sister Anna, the nun in charge approached me.

"Can I skip confession today? I already prayed the rosary with my mother before I came to school. And I tripped, look! My knee is bleeding." Raised my leg to show her the wound.

Sister Anna handed me a handkerchief. "Confession is an integral part of our belief. Your sins must be forgiven by the grace of God so you can heal."

"Do you mean prayers can heal my wounded knee?" I asked, trying to be the smarty-pants.

She snapped at me. "Your wound will heal, but your sins won't be forgiven unless you confess."

Loud murmurs erupted.

"Hush." Sister Anna glared at my classmates.

"Do I only confess my sins or my father's sins as well?" I asked. "They picked up my father!"

"I know about your father. That's why you need to go to confession for you and your father's sins," Sister Anna persisted. "Stay in line now."

Desperate to leave, I wiped the blood off my knee with Sister Anna's handkerchief while waiting for my turn to confess.

Moments later and with hesitation, I stepped inside the confession box, knelt, and made the sign of the cross. "Bless me Father for I have sinned."

"What are your sins?" The priest asked.

I cleared my throat. "My father was a sinner, and I inherited his sins."

Are sins passed on genetically?

"I am condemned from the guilt and the shame of being my father's daughter," I choked in between tears.

"Just pray three Our Father's and three Hail Mary's my child."

"That's all?" *Can't believe this.* "Do you think prayers will wipe away the sins embedded in me?" Raised my voice.

"Child, ple – "

Rising from the pedestal I barged outside and without looking back, I broke into a sprint.

The other kids stared at me with a mixture of pity and disdain. "Her father is a criminal," they whispered. "He's in prison now; serves him right!"

I ran 'til reaching the school gate. The guard stopped me in my tracks and prohibited me from leaving the campus without Sister Anna's instruction. Squatting on the floor, I embraced my knees and curled up in a ball of defeat.

Convulsing in tears, I said, "Da…Daddy, they have taken my Daddy away."

9 DENIAL

December 1972

Wounds still fresh from dad's arrest, my family and I gathered at the dinner table, but this time with no more jokes and banter. Mom's dark and gloomy mood hovered around us as she picked on her food in stony silence like she was transported into a different realm.

Breaking the silence, I blurted out, "Mom, is Dad a gangster?"

"Why would do you ask that?" Mom raised her eyebrows and it seemed like my question jolted her back into this world. "He's on a business trip, remember?"

I couldn't believe she was denying it.

"No, Mom. Dad got arrested. It's all over school and everyone is talking about it." I slammed the table. "Why aren't you telling the truth?

Mom looked me in the eye, opened her lips as if to say something, then clammed up, escaping into her imaginary world.

We ate in silence, and then retreated to our bedrooms. The hole in my heart grew bigger as the days unfolded. My childhood had been ripped out, and to me, this was the point of no return.

When the news broke that my father had been arrested and jailed as a conspirator to a planned assassination of President Marcos, my low self-esteem fell to new depths. I felt like 'the cursed child' reeking of body odor and bad breath that everyone avoided. I was the girl singled out for the awful hair in shampoo commercials; that despite the daily dose of coconut milk my mother applied to it. My insecurities grew, and I desperately wanted to quit school.

"Everyone's avoiding me," I complained to my mom, who thought I was exaggerating. "When I'm with my schoolmates, they become quiet then scatter like crows!" I was sure they were talking about me. My imagination wandered to every dark possibility and built the foundation for my deep inferiority complex at a very early age.

I later realized that my mother was going through the same emotional havoc that I was experiencing. She anxiously waited for any news about Dad's whereabouts and was on a phone vigil just in case he called. I overheard her talking to one of her friends on the phone pleading, "Where is he? Heaven help me!"

Worry was engraved on her pretty face as she'd pray for divine intervention, "Blessed Mary, where is my husband? Please keep him safe."

She was right to be worried about his safety. With Martial Law in full force, rumors spread about people being arrested and then disappearing forever. "What am I going to do?" My mom asked her friends. "How am I going to go on without him?" Though her friends would reassure her that everything would be okay, his absence dominated our lives at home and in the community.

As the days unfolded and when Dad was permitted a phone call to us, he echoed the same consoling tone. "Everything is going to be all right! I'll be out of here soon," he'd tell Mom to instruct us. "Be good kids and listen to your mother and don't give her too much trouble."

We wanted to believe him so badly and hoped that he was telling the truth, but beneath our young minds was the fear that we may never see him again.

This fear lived in my nightly dreams.

We'd watch popular TV series that showed bloody combat scenes of violence; prisoners of war screamed as they were clobbered and beaten bloody. If they were not tortured, they were executed.

Night after night, I would hear voices screaming in pain. "Help us, you have the keys. Write about us, tell them what you see." I dreamt of detainees being beaten, electrocuted, hanged, raped, humiliated, and mutilated. I dreamt of the lines of civilians facing the walls, soldiers raising their rifles pointed at their backs, detainees looking up to heaven and inhaling their last breathes... and *Bang!* I'd wake up screaming and sweating.

But, in the light of day we spoke the language of denial. We pretended that Dad was just on one of his frequent business trips and life went on as usual. "Dads in Manila," was my quick response when asked where he was. "You see, he's running a construction business there. He will be back soon," I'd mimic my mom's reactions.

***

I learned many years later that right after Dad was arrested, they took him to a police station on Jones Avenue, now called Osmeña Boulevard, and held him there in the notorious detention center of the Marcos Regime located in Cebu. The center housed the Philippine Constabulary, with a dual function of serving as both military and police headquarters. Marcos used this institution to arrest and hold political dissenters. Much later, when Cory Aquino was elected

President of the Philippines, the Constabulary was dissolved. We all worried about what might happen to Dad in this infamous prison. Many years later he told me my worries weren't unfounded.

"Because of your Tito Barry, I was treated well at the barracks," Dad had explained to me several years later when I asked him about it. "The guards offered me cigarettes when I first got there, and I received a decent bed to sleep in. I was not handcuffed when they picked me up."

Dad had been gone for a month when we learned he'd been moved to Manila, an hour's flight north of Cebu on the island of Luzon. We had an apartment in Manila, and upon his arrival, he was given a few days pass to contemplate the final days of freedom he'd known for many years. Dad later told me that he'd thanked Tito Barry for giving him those precious hours, even though he had been the instrument in Dad's arrest. As soon as Tito Barry had heard about Dad's impending arrest, he immediately volunteered to place him under his custody to soften the blow or perhaps to provide him a shield of protection.

After that respite, my father was required to turn himself over to the Presidential Security Command Headquarters at the Malacañang Palace compound in Manila. Malacañang Palace was our "White House," where President Marcos and his family lived and ruled over the country.

When Mom discovered where Dad was, she immediately flew to Manila with my grandmother, Mama Lingling. Upon arrival at the Palace, they were told that the prisoners were not allowed to have visitors at that time. Because Mama Lingling, had an influential network whose strings she was adept at pulling, she'd expected to be admitted. But the trip was in vain, and they returned to Cebu discouraged and worried.

"This was very painful to me," Dad recalled. The word 'prisoner' was finally sinking in and becoming very real for us all. The stigma of Dad's incarceration haunted us at home as neighbors and the community sat in judgment. Concern for Dad's safety and well-being dominated our daily life.

But worries about the conditions of Dad's imprisonment did not match up to reality. He continued to be detained at an Annex building of the luxurious Malacañang Palace. He and the other prisoners were housed in VIP air-conditioned rooms, complete with televisions; they continued to smoke their blue-seal Winston Cigarettes, drink their imported instant coffee (Taster's Choice), and contraband Johnny Walker and Chivas Regal. They were also allowed to visit the chapel on the Malacañang grounds. Dad was housed among his famous and infamous political friends who had previously been mayors, senators, and governors from their respective districts.

"Mrs. Josefa Marcos, the President's mother, walked the grounds daily and went to the chapel to pray." Dad later told me. "Sometimes, we sat on the same bench."

Finally, after several months of detention, families were allowed to visit. Spouses brought specialty foods and delicacies requested by their imprisoned loved ones. Except for missing their families, daily life was quite comfortable for my dad and his fellow detainees. The same was not true for my mother.

Dad later recounted the anxiety she possessed, worrying aloud about her children she'd had to leave at home in the care of a series of *yayas* and her agonizing about our family's income. She was particularly concerned about my father's existing construction company.

"What are we going to do about your business?" Mom fretted.

Dad had more than one hundred employees and as soon as they had learned that Dad was not coming back anytime soon, many looted his offices and disappeared. Others were loyal and faithfully continued working without a paycheck for several months at a time.

Many years later, I asked Larry, Dad's right-hand man, and most loyal employee, "Why did you stick with Dad, even when you were not paid a salary?"

He spoke fondly of my father. "Your Dad was extremely strict. It was always a roller coaster ride working with your Dad," he said. "We would go months with no paycheck, but when your dad was able to collect funds from the government, he was generous and gave us fat bonuses. It was well worth it to stick around."

I too remember the financial yo-yos of those days swinging from feast to famine. We were lean for several months, and suddenly one day we would wake up to find a brand-new Mercedes parked in our garage, Dad's dream car.

"Why don't you lease a house here near Manila, so you'd be closer to me?" Dad responded to Mom's anxieties. "The children need to wrap-up school. They'll be safe and secure at home with the governess Nang' Felisa," Dad had suggested so Mom wouldn't be burdened with frequent travel between the islands.

Mom took his advice. This eased her emotional and financial strain. While Nang' Felisa would look after us in Cebu, Mom made sure we still had a roof over our heads, food on the table, and that we were well-behaved. The plan was that my siblings and I would visit Dad in Manila during our vacations from school.

In theory, it sounded like the perfect plan, and looking back, I could not find the words to describe what I was going through, and had to deal with, with the fate that was handed me. I learned to live day-by-day and obliterate a past not to my liking. Today, I am collecting the fragments in my life and piecing them together to make sense of it all. I've been unmasking the thick cloak of denial that I have harbored for so many years.

The tapestry continues to unravel while the story unfolds.

10 THE INTERVIEW

July 2007

Hoping to improve my craft in writing and meet fellow writers in Benicia, I joined a writer's group during the summer. We were eight attendees that met once a week with Ralph, the leader in one of the conference rooms at the local library.

Ralph, a stocky, older man crowned in voluminous white hair radiated a warm smile. "Welcome."

I proceeded to the corner of the room and mingled with the other attendees.

Ralph laid out the rules for the group and gave us a brief background about himself. "I wanted to share the good news. I recently won first prize in a contest for the essay I submitted about my ten years of incarceration in California."

Claps filled the air.

"Congratulations." I spoke.

Ralph beamed with pride. "Thank you, everyone. The price is $65,000 worth of scholarship in an MFA program at St. Mary's in Moraga.

"Wow!" the group gasped in amazement.

After getting to know him and the other group members, we wrapped up our introductions with an assignment, an essay about any topic close to our heart.

I could not wait to jot down all my thoughts and feelings about my childhood trauma as if to purge it all on paper. We wrote in silence; I felt relieved and cleansed after writing several pages about Dad and our family.

We submitted our essays the following week; one writer was assigned each week to read what they had written.

After my turn, Ralph took me aside. "You got a story in there," he said. "I would encourage you to write a book about it."

"I have always wanted to," I said. "It's my dream."

"If you want, I can help you," Ralph offered.

"I would love that," I said. "I'm afraid, Dad is not exactly forthright with me. It's been very painful for him, and he'd rather not talk about it."

***

Dad happened to be visiting California at that time, and I was excited to tell him the news when I got home.

"Hey Dad, guess what?" I asked him while greeting him with a peck on the cheek.

"What's up?" He asked with eyebrows raised.

"Ralph is interested in your story, and he thinks it would make a great book!"

"Really?"

"Yes, he would like to interview you, while you are here."

"Sure, let's do it!"

We met that afternoon, in a tiny, cozy coffee shop by the marina.

Ralph, Dad, and I sipped coffee and ate our scones while engaging in light conversation about golf and the weather before we dove the purpose of the meeting.

Seagulls fluttered into the tranquil water while the flawless sun radiated from the surface.

Being a history graduate, I was inquisitive and never stopped asking questions about everything.

Dad was receptive to all my questions except when he talked about his own experience in prison.

"I don't like talking about that chapter in my life, too many painful memories that I prefer to bury. If this were not for my daughter's request, I wouldn't be here now." He winked.

In support of my quest for answers, I appealed to Ralph to conduct an interview while I pulled out my mini recorder; I set it on the table and pressed the red button. Together, we were able to stitch Dad's story. That initial exchange went something like this:

Ralph: So how did you get arrested?

Dad: It was ASSO (Arrest, Search and Seizure Order), do you know what that is?

This was the first time I heard of that, I learned something new that day.

Ralph: Yes, of course.

Dad: That's what they did.

Ralph: So, they found all these weapons in your room?

Dad: Yes!

Ralph: What kind of weapons?

Dad: Everything, Walter, Thompson machine guns... you name it.

Ralph: Wow! (Chuckled)

Dad: It was necessary. Our lives were in danger.

Ralph: How many were arrested?

Dad: We were about twenty-six people. They had to arrest all of us to conjure a conspiracy.

Ralph: How long were you in?

Dad: Four and half years.

From the interview, I had learned that for four months Dad had remained in the Malacañang Palace with twenty-six other detainees until they were all moved to Fort Bonifacio, where most political prisoners were eventually sent.

Fort Bonifacio was a distinctive place noted for its plush housing units occupied by favored retired military officers and for its pristine golf course and cemetery. However, there was another far less comfortable section of the fort where prisoners like my father were held—political enemies of President Marcos, and even some of his friends, as well as his many businesses and economic rivals. Most were not subversives but were nonetheless taken into custody under Martial Law to prevent potential dissidents from organizing against the 'New Order' imposed by the Marcos Regime. Their confinement at the fort was not as comfortable as the

Malacañang Palace and featured smaller jail cells, concrete floors, an open sink and toilet, and iron bars on doors and windows.

It was in the scandalous Fort Bonifacio prison that my father witnessed the cruelty of Martial Law. He told me about the many notable people who kept him company in those difficult and uncertain years. Some eventually made it to freedom while others did not, depending on their financial resources and political influences.

Among them was Senator Benigno Aquino Jr., known as Ninoy, who earned his way into the hearts and history of the Filipino people. He was a staunch critic of Ferdinand Marcos and his policies. Ninoy never wavered, not even while held in solitary confinement where he went on lengthy hunger strikes. Despite deteriorating health, Ninoy's trial was held, and in 1977 he was sentenced to death by a military commission for the crimes of subversion and murder.

Ralph: So Ninoy Aquino was in the same cell as you?

Dad: We were in the same compound, but he was in a different cell. He was isolated from all of us.

"Why, Dad?" I asked.

Dad: Ninoy was such a charismatic and brilliant talker that they felt the need to isolate him. He probably could talk his way out of jail by charming the guards. We were all in solitary confinement for a couple of months, but Ninoy remained there the whole time. He was a serious threat to Marcos.

Ralph: "Did he escape?"

Dad: Kinda', I think they just let him go. They probably had an arrangement, who knows? He had a stroke, and the First Lady Imelda Marcos came to visit him. Imelda allowed him to travel to the US for surgery if he promised not to form a resistance abroad.

Ninoy had little faith in promises from Marcos and after recovering from surgery; he requested political asylum in the United States. He used this time as Marcos had feared—to speak against the regime and rally support.

By 1983, Ninoy had become extremely concerned about worsening political and social conditions in the Philippines. Although strongly warned by the First Lady Imelda Marcos and his supporters that returning to his homeland would be a death sentence, Ninoy boarded a plane, famously declaring, 'The Filipinos are worth dying for.' His plane landed at the Manila airport, and Ninoy stepped out onto the tarmac where he was immediately cut down by an assassin's bullet. Millions of people rallied on the streets across the Philippine Islands to mourn the loss of a national hero.

Ninoy's example created a groundswell in the country and grew into the People's Power Movement that included millions of grassroots activists and supporters from all over the Philippines. It culminated many years later with the return of Ninoy's widow, Corazon 'Cory' Aquino, who, despite her lack of political experience, was elected President of the Philippines in 1986. The legacy of Ninoy further extended to his son, Senator Benigno Aquino III, who leveraged the family name and also became President of the Philippines in 2010.

The interview lingered on into the afternoon.

"Dad and Ralph do you guys want more coffee?" I asked.

"No, I am good," Dad said.

Ralph shook his head and continued the interview.

Dad relayed more info about the Plaza Miranda Bombing:

"Boom!" A big bang exploded in the Plaza Miranda rally, just when the liberal party formed a line, held hands, and raised their arms in victory.

"Bomba!" The frightened people yelled as they huddled to attend the rally. The Liberal Party of the Philippines launched a political campaign at the Plaza

Miranda in the district of Quiapo, Manila on August 21, 1971. Free speech was encouraged as it was considered a center for political discourse. The Liberal Party's campaign rally was held to announce the candidacies of eight Senatorial bets as well as the candidate for the Mayoral Race in Manila.

"AAAaaaaaaaahhhhh, tulong," the masses screamed as a crowd of about four thousand people dispersed. They came to hear speeches from their favorite candidates, peek at celebrity guests, and enjoy some entertainment, but then two hand grenades were reportedly tossed on stage.

"Dios ko," were the outcries of the people that scrambled. Many were injured as the crowd spread and they ran for safety. The incident tolled nine deaths and injured ninety-five others, including many prominent Liberal Party politicians.

Mita: Were you present during the bombing?

Dad: No, thank God. I was visiting your brothers in the US. If I were in the Philippines, for sure I would be hurt as well.

Ralph: What is the Plaza Miranda bombing?

Mita: Plaza Miranda was a place in Manila, a center for political discourse. The liberal party held a rally to declare the candidacies of the liberal party while two hand grenades were thrown at the podium. Nine people were killed, and many were injured.

Dad: Serging was heavily injured and nearly died. He was paralyzed and temporarily confined to a wheelchair.

Mita: Dad, do you think that the NPA's were involved?

Dad: Marcos blamed the NPA's as well as the student activists who regularly picketed in front of the Malacañang Palace and their universities, rallying for a just social system.

Ralph: What's the NPA?

Mita: It's the New People's Army. They are the armed wing of the communist party in the Philippines. Most of them are based in the countryside. I believe they were more hungry than principled.

Dad: The ambush of Enrile, that was a setup too!

Ralph: Who is Enrile?

Mita: Juan Ponce Enrile served as the Justice Secretary and Defense Minister during Martial Law.

Dad: They had nothing on me, except being a friend of Serging.

Mita: Then why did they arrest you, Dad?

Dad: You see, it was easier to arrest all of us and accused us of conspiracy rather than arrest us separately and then making a case against us individually.

The Plaza Miranda incident, as well as the rising presence of the resistance group, the National People's Army (NPA's) and student activists clamoring for a social change, as well as the ambush of Secretary of Defense, Enrile's car, random bombings in Manila, and other large cities, supplied the pretext for the declaration of martial law on September 21, 1972. Many people believe that those events were rigged, that President Marcos had planned it all along to proclaim Martial Law, he had been preparing the country for an autocratic government even before the decree.

The Osmeñas

In 1969, when Serging ran against incumbent President Marcos, Dad stepped up to support his friend and colleague:

Ralph: What about Serging Osmeña, Jr?

Dad: He was a good friend of mine. In 1969, he ran for president against the incumbent Marcos, and I helped him with his campaign.

Mita: Was he the mayor of Cebu, Dad?

Dad: Serging used to be the Governor of Cebu, and then became a mayor, a congressman, and eventually a senator.

Mita: (Looked at Ralph) Serging's father, Sergio Osmeña Sr. served as President of the Philippines during the American Commonwealth period from 1944 to 1946.

Giving Ralph a brief synopsis of Philippine History, Dad continued.

The late Senator Sergio "Serging" Osmeña Jr. was also a powerful force in the country. Serging came from the wealthy gentry, with a rich family history of politics and patriotism. President Osmeña Sr. waded ashore with General Douglas MacArthur upon his return to the Philippines with his historic slogan, 'I shall return!'

Ralph: Wow, this is interesting! Did they arrest Serging Osmeña, Jr. as well?

Dad: As I said, Serging was severely injured in the Plaza Miranda incident in 1971. Serging traveled to the United States to receive medical treatment. He was out of the country when Martial Law was declared.

Mita: Oh, I thought you were in Fort Bonifacio with them. I heard the Osmeñas were also detained.

Dad: That is right. They arrested his son, Serge Osmeña, and his nephew, Lito Osmeña instead.

Ralph: How did you get to know Serging?

Dad: My mother attended the same private boarding school, Assumption College in Manila, as did Serging's mother, Estafania. I met Serging through my mother. Mama made the phone call and introduced us. We even found out that we were related.

Dad explained that he and Serging shared the same biological lineage from an affluent Cebuano family of Chinese descent. The children of such relationships were born out of wedlock and never bore the name of their grandfather, an influential man in Cebu who fulfilled his responsibility by making certain all his children received the proper education and were well cared for.

Mita: What was he like, Dad?

Dad: When we met in person, we hit it off immediately because I was funny and Serging was a profoundly serious man. Serging had a magnetic personality about him that attracted people. I remember he also had a warm heart and couldn't refuse a request for help. He was such a soft touch that eventually people were hired to protect him from those folks who wanted to take advantage of his generous nature.

Ralph: Did you run for a political position too?

Dad: Yes, I did twice in 1965 and 1969 but I lost. In 1969, I played an active role in supporting Osmeña. I raised funds for his 1969 election. I raised 20 million Pesos for his campaign, and he was appreciative. The money for Osmeña's presidential bid was a pledge by an anonymous Sultan from Sabah, Borneo. The Sultan was my golf buddy from Brunei.

It was a complicated and covert contribution; Dad met a shipping tycoon who served as the Liberal Party's treasurer in Hong Kong where the campaign cash was handed over in a briefcase. I remember those briefcases, one brother claimed. "I would go to the dad's room and see these briefcases of cash. "I easily swipe wads of cash without anyone noticing," one of my older brothers said.

Stories like this one and my dad's recollections of Fort Bonifacio and his fellow inmates fascinated me.

Inside Fort Bonifacio

Mita: (Facing Ralph) I remembered our visits to him well, but we were never allowed to enter the facility. We were brought to an amphitheater on the property, so we didn't know what was going on inside.

Dad: Yes, they were extremely strict indeed.

Mita: Our visits began after the school year ended and my sister Candy, my older brother, Jake and I had temporarily just moved to Manila. We were able to visit Dad with Mom once a week. We had to sign in at the security gate. A military jeep picked us up from the security checkpoint and drove us along an open field to the amphitheater.

Ralph: What did you do when you got there?

Mita: We brought a lot of food as if we were going to a picnic. We were always tense and nervous. Later on, we were more relaxed as we got to know other detainees and their children as well. There was always friendly banter among the detainees and their families.

Dad: The hardest part for me was missing Christmas, birthdays, and graduations.

Mita: Yes, Dad. It was awfully hard for us too.

Wives, unaccustomed to the role of being head of the family, were required to step up to new demands while continuing to provide the nurturing expected of them as mothers and spouses. Children in families like ours seldom understood what had happened to their patriarchs and were left to cope on their own. The political prisoners went overnight from being lives of privilege to daily deprivation. The strong, like my father and many of the prisoners who had adapted and survived one day at a time, emerged to fight to rebuild their previous stature. Nonetheless, years of absence from family life exact a toll on everyone; particularly children whose lives changed almost overnight.

That Fort Bonifacio had a history was small comfort. It was originally named Fort McKinley in 1901, during the Philippine- American War. In 1949, it was returned to the Philippine government and renamed Fort Bonifacio, after the Filipino hero who led the 1890s movement to gain independence from Spain. Andres Bonifacio was the 'Supremo' of the Katipunan, the Philippine revolutionary society that upended the status quo. He is known as "The father of the Philippine Revolution" and gave his life for the cause. He was executed in 1897.

Paradoxically, during the thirty-plus years of Martial Law under President Ferdinand Marcos, the character of Fort Bonifacio changed. It went from being a symbol of military strength and defense named in honor of a Philippine rebel and hero, to a detention center for dissident against the Marcos Regime.

I took a deep breath as the sun cascaded in. Dad seemed tired, but I was relieved the meeting was productive. I did not realize the depth of what he had to go through all these years ago. My selfish needs seemed immaterial.

Mita: Dad, are you okay?

Dad: I am going to be okay. My deepest regret in life is not being able to spend time with you and your brothers and sister.

Mita: This was never your fault, Dad. You never asked for this.

Dad: I filed a suit in Hawaii as part of the Reparation Act. Even if I don't see a cent, I was hoping that you or your children would at least get something from it.

Mita: Dad, don't worry about it.

I gently laid my hand on his shoulder. Thank you for sharing this with us, Dad. It means so much to me.

Ralph: Thank you so much for sharing Mr. Zara. You indeed have an amazing story that needs to be shared with the world.

I pressed the stop button of the recorder while Dad and Ralph shook hands. I realized how this fateful afternoon allowed me to peek inside Dad's world during his captivity. My father had been through so much and my purpose is to sow the seeds of this book so I can share our story with the world.

11 THE WRITER

March 1974

Mom was mostly based in Manila to be closer to Dad while he was in prison, but she found time to pay a short visit to Cebu.

We gathered at the dining table eating *Tableya*, *puto*, and ripe yummy mangos for *merienda*. If only this dining table could talk, there would be so many stories it could tell; this table had witnessed our joys, laments, and our silence.

"Oh, this is yummy!" Mom said, relishing every morsel from the sweet rice cake and guzzling it down with hot chocolate.

Watching her eat with delight made me miss her more. With the weary look she exuded, Mom embraced a simpler outfit—a leisurely free flowing *Batik* duster dress which was a far cry from the socialite I knew a couple of years ago. The once elegant woman dressed up in the finest *haute couture* and her hair fashionably done by a personal *friseur was now pale and stricken with worry.* I absorbed the layers of anxiety and pain beneath her stoic lovely face.

"How are you? What's been going on?" Mom asked.

"I am okay, Mom." I learned to use a generic response to all the situations I was confronted with even if I was panic-laden and in deep pain. I inherited Mom's stoicism. If she can do it, so can I. "When are you flying back?"

"Tomorrow." Mom took a sip of water.

I froze as a shot of sorrow permeated all over my body.

Oh no, she's leaving again! What about me?

Unable to eat, I toyed with the plate of snacks in front of me. Choking in between tears, I took a huge gulp of the cup of warm chocolate, hoping the sugar will drown my sorrows and transport me to a world of bliss.

"Yes, tomorrow." Mom stared into space again like she was in denial of the situation.

My lips quivered, then chocolate spilled on my shirt. *Shit!*

Mom didn't seem to notice and all I wanted was to wrap my arms around her in a tight embrace, but I chose to keep my composure in the hopes that I could be strong like her.

My only solace in those dark months was for the first time communicating with Dad. I wrote him letters that mom delivered to him during her frequent visits to the prison.

"Make sure you hand me your letters to your dad, so I can take them with me. They don't allow any reading materials inside the prison except for the Bible," Mom always reminded me when she was around. "He looks forward to your letters."

"What should I write about, Mom?" I asked.

"Just write about anything, I am sure he will be glad to hear from you. He's always asking about you."

After snacks, I excused myself and headed to my bedroom where I could write Dad a letter. Spending time alone with Mom meant so much to me.

The chair wobbled as I scribbled over and over again. How should a daughter of a prisoner tell him that I am overwhelmed with sorrow, and I can't seem to translate it on paper? Tears trickled down my cheeks allowing the pen to take a life of its own.

Dear Dad,

Hope you are okay. Are they treating you well?

I'm doing my best to keep busy in school, but still don't know what degree I want to pursue in college.

However, playing chess with my cousins next door also occupies my time. Aside from that, I have improved my skills in table tennis, which has allowed me to be a part of the varsity team and represent our school. I am also learning to play tennis and becoming quite good at it.

Dad, can you help me decide what I should take up in college? Did you know what you were going to be at my age?

As I continued to write to Dad about my doubts and interests, he wrote back with comforting words: "You're still young. You will find your way. It just takes time."

I wrote to him as a pen pal, as a confessor, and receiving a letter from him always put a smile on my face.

I don't know what I'm going to be when I grow up. I have an interest in something and then later just lose interest. Is something wrong with me?

He was very understanding and wrote: *Don't worry, that's normal.*

His response helped me feel better. I needed some sense of normal in my life.

I enjoyed the letter exchanges with Dad. For the first time in my life, I was getting to know him. He was responding and paying more attention to and this is what I craved. I wrote to him about everything—about my goals and what I wanted out of life. And his responses were just what I had wanted from a father. Ironically, Dad's captivity bridged the gap between us.

From that moment on, writing letters to my father proved to be my salvation. I learned much later that the letters we shared were as much an epiphany for him as they were for me. It seemed he hadn't known me until we corresponded through our letters. In one of our correspondence, I told him that I had decided to be a writer.

My father, wondering why his business ambition had skipped a generation in his family, discouraged me.

There's no money in that, how about being a doctor?

No, Dad, I'd faint from a drop of blood! I responded.

Okay, then. What about being a nurse?

He persisted. *My father was a doctor, but I didn't have the money to become a doctor. I worked my way through college instead, to become an engineer. My brothers became doctors because my mother supported them.*

I believe because of this inequity; he fantasized that one of his kids would become a doctor or a nurse; someone who could at least take care of him in his old age. I suspected it was every Filipino father's fantasy.

But that was not me, I always knew I was going to be a writer one day. I would edit my missives a hundred times over until I was mentally drained, and my hand ached from scribbling. I wrote to Dad to amuse him since no magazines or newspapers were allowed in his cell, but our letters went through. Every time I wrote to Dad or someone else, I poured my heart, body, and soul into it, and all my energy flowed from my fingers into the pen and ultimately in that piece of paper until I was exhausted and fell asleep. I was always surprised at what I'd written, feeling like a different personality had taken over and finished writing the letters while I slept. I arose to hundreds of stories of love, betrayal, tragedy, comedy, and of characters who I did not even know. *Did I write this?*

Although I produced hundreds of letters, I only sent him a few. I hesitated to send them for fear that he would misunderstand me. Usually, my letters took on a life of their own and ended up like a cliché'—*happily ever after*, was my favorite tagline. Wherein Dad would never have been arrested and Mom would be in the kitchen, cooking and baking up a storm for the entire family, while dogs barked in the background. We would all be eating, laughing, loving, and playing our usual pranks at each other. We would be happy, carefree with no troubles. This was the alternative universe I'd create.

Writing was an escape from my current reality, that of becoming a Physical Education teacher since I was active in Ping-Pong, tennis, and swimming. I also enjoyed ballet and karate classes. However, I loved the feeling of being so tired that I could daydream before sleeping.

Dad and I continued to communicate about the present and my future. He didn't like either option I had chosen for my future. He still encouraged me to aspire to a profession that might better provide for my family. Even though there was no harsh judgment about my choices, the rebel in me persisted.

I handed the letter to Mom and kissed her on the cheek. "Have a safe trip."

She forced a smile then exited the front door leaving me again in my alternate universe.

The letter exchanges with Dad were a lifeline for a lonely, frightened, teenage girl grasping in the dark for a logical meaning of her reality. Writing saved my soul. From the pit of my stomach, I knew it was my calling.

12 COLLEGE

March 1975

After graduating from high school, I moved to Manila in the following year to pursue my college education.

"I don't know what I will take up, Mom," I said, pressured into making a life decision.

"How about Business?" Mom suggested. "Your brother took that course. You should be good at it too."

"I want you to take the course that your heart desires," Dad said.

What was my heart's desire? I just longed for my family to be all together again. Was it wrong?

My family encouraged me to study business at the university because this was the only course my family was comfortable with. The entrepreneurial spirit streamed into my family's veins. However, my mental capacity was not compatible with numbers and figures. Unlike my father who had a photographic memory, he retained numbers and captured a snapshot of calculations in one glance.

I preferred the Arts. I suspect this was one of the reasons he was a successful engineer, although he would have wanted to be a doctor. His mathematical genius was particularly handy especially when he prepared quotes to bid for a large project like estimating the costs that go with developing bridges, roads, buildings, subdivision, or reclaiming chunks of land.

Since I was drowning in the maze and principles of business courses, I decided to switch to Liberal Arts and majored in Asian Studies at De La Salle University. We studied Japanese and Chinese history, which I could very much identify with. I suspected that I have these Asian imprints in my DNA.

During our summer break, I looked forward to spending my vacations in Cebu.

Eager to be back, I stood in front of my childhood home assessing the structure noting how it had survived the wear and tear of external forces, as well as the spirits of all itinerant borders and the ghosts that have been passing through. The exterior white paint was chipping off and stained by the weather. As I stepped inside the premises, the elaborate wood-carved door looked sturdy but old and dusty. The marble showed signs of visible cracks and dents. Despite the structural mishaps, home was still where the heart is. This was the only home I had ever known, and I was glad to be here.

After all the welcome greetings from the maids, I headed to my pink bedroom adorned with wallflower of roses and petals and matching pink flowery curtains. Nancy, my precious talking doll was still a fixture in my bed. I hugged her, "Oh Nancy, it's so good to be home."

I plopped on my bed and wiggled my toes.

Moments later, the maid handed me the cordless phone. "Ma'am, *si* Lally."

Lally, my favorite cousin chirped. "Welcome back."

"Yeah, how are you? Want to meet up for coffee?"

"I can't! I am working," Lally said.

I leaned over to look at the calendar. "Oh, cool, so we need to catch up soon then. When are you free?"

"Not for the time being. Listen, I work at Cathay Pacific and Northwest office and need to leave for Manila tomorrow. They need to hire someone to replace me. It's just a summer job, would you be interested?"

And although the thought of working intimidated me, I agreed.

This was the first time I'd worked and earned a decent wage outside of the family business and I enjoyed the feeling of independence. I decided to stay in Cebu and finish up my studies at the University of San Carlos. They did not offer Asian studies but instead World History. Europe was considered the old World, but it was like a different planet to me, and I couldn't relate to their history. Instead, I just dreamt about these places I had read about, and I longed to see the world. The seeds of "wanderlust" had been sown.

I graduated with a degree in Liberal Arts with a major in History. It was not a coincidence that I am now dealing with the history of the Philippines and my family. Looking back, my childhood was divided by the distinct timeline drawn by the declaration of Martial Law.

After my father was taken away, money quickly became an issue for the family at home. Mom sold almost everything of valuable we'd owned except for the house, which she had considered as an option, but Dad forbade her from doing so.

Indeed, our house was unique. At one time, it was featured in a local architectural magazine as one of the best houses of the 1960s. Dad was not ready to let go of it, in part, because it symbolized the pinnacle of his business success and it was a unique, custom-built home designed by my uncle, Tito Bob.

It was a three-thousand-square-foot, 'L-shaped' structure with one entire side featuring glass doors instead of walls. At one time in the 60s, those glass walls were considered 'mod'. It looked stunning but presented the constant danger of someone walking or running right into the glass. I witnessed many such accidents while growing up in that house. We would hear a loud "BANG," and someone howling in pain. As kids that would always make us giggle mischievously. Those same glass doors allowed people to see right into our lives. I felt like we were living in an aquarium.

With a new determination to be a writer, I made it a habit to keep a journal and write at least an hour a day. One evening at dusk, after dinner, I settled at my writing desk and scribbled about the days' events recording my thoughts, and before I knew it, I felt the earth under my feet move. My desk with my hand on my journal began shaking. I looked at the walls, and the picture frames were dancing, and the whole room was swirling. Shaken to my core, my heart raced with cold chills running through my spine. I was paralyzed. *Bang!*

Am I dead or alive?

The loud noise of shattered glass penetrated the walls. I waited for it to be all over and realized we had just had an earthquake. I held Nancy close to my beating heart and hugged her tight.

"We are going to be okay, Nancy," I said, "We'll get through this."

With Nancy attached to my chest, I stormed out of the room joining my neighbors, cousins, and siblings who were recuperating from the scene at the living room.

"Careful," Manny said. "There's lots of broken glass. Tread lightly."

Splintered glass occupied the floor, picture frames and vases were relocated, and floor cracks stretched to the end of the hall.

All my cousins, neighbors, uncles, aunts, and helpers were outside, hugging one another.

"That was an earthquake, glad we are all safe."

We learned that the earthquake was an intensity of 8.0 hits Cebu and the surrounding islands with no fatalities.

Still shaken about what happened, the earthquake proved to be a symbol of my life — broken and hopeless.

Days turned into weeks and as soon as summer ended, Mom rebuilt the house in time for Dad to return from his captivity. She chose a Mediterranean style featuring decorative steel wall panels instead of glass doors that allowed a cool breeze to pass through during hot, humid, tropical days. The wrought iron minimized accidents, compared to the glass doors, but people could still view our misery and pain from the outside —it was an invasion of privacy.

Gripping the wrought iron barrier, I drew in a breath, harboring the wretched life and misery we all shared. *Oh my God, what must Dad be thinking? This feels like I'm in prison.*

Although the iron grills felt confined, there was so much more that was unique and wonderful about the home I remember. There was a huge backyard that I loved. Dad had built a practice putting green; he even included sand traps. "Your putting determines your victory," he would say, sharing his philosophy of golf (and life) with us.

Our home also featured a unique swimming pool with a tunnel that connected to the living room and flowed into the master bedroom. As children, we splashed all over the living area when we dove into the pool and happily swam. And, when we had a chance, we playfully pushed our friends into the pool. When my brothers were old enough to hold house parties, they specialized in this family trick, nudging guests over the edge at every opportunity. Our life was filled with such mischief and pranks.

***

As I write this story decades later, a smile always plays on my lips. We were a wild bunch then with so many memories. My cousins and my siblings would gather at the house and wrestled. We had safe harmless plastic swords and other toy weapons, fenced with one another, pushed one another playfully. We beat up each other with soft pillows to steam off some aggression. However, one such incident became dangerous when someone pushed my sister Candy into the pool that had been emptied of water for maintenance.

Silence filled the air before Manny cried, "*Tabang*! Mom, help! Candy just fell."

Frantic, Mom pleaded. "Call Adrian, the doctor." She meant an uncle next door who was still a medical student.

I scrambled to my feet. "Mom, he's not a doctor yet. He's an intern."

Candy was rushed to the hospital. No one knew exactly what happened. It happened so fast. Everyone felt guilty and took the blame.

After the tragedy, Mom decided to seal the tunnel from the pool.

They closed the opening in the living room as well as the opening that led to my parent's bedroom. It was fun while it lasted. Many years later, I would still meet friends who would remember our house and the marvelous water tunnel. I can understand why Dad was determined not to lose our remarkable home. Despite the tragedies, I retained bittersweet memories in my heart.

After Dad's arrest, in the absence of his income and our mother's constant presence, the house was no longer what it once was. It just remained a skeletal structure of what it used to be; its life and joy sucked out of it. Perhaps most telling was what happened to that amazing swimming pool.

Before the arrest, we had a pool guy who maintained it on a regular schedule as well as our garden that was accentuated by the green grass surrounding the pool. But after the arrest, we couldn't afford the upkeep, the chemicals required to clean it and the laborers. The water was drained from the pool. In the beginning, my brothers and cousins explored creative endeavors with their electric guitars and other musical instruments and jammed in the empty pool as the acoustics amplified their music and provided them with some fun. Eventually, the fun wore off and the empty concrete pool was just another reminder of our problem.

Since we lived near a dried creek and the pool was no longer being cared for, bright green moss emerged on the tiles, attracting an army of happy frogs. They migrated to the pool in droves, bringing family and friends.

Ku-kak, ku-kak, the frogs croaked their symphony every night, disturbing our slumber. Our pool was no longer a luxury or a pleasure. It became a sanctuary for hopping, croaking amphibians – it was worthy of selling admission tickets to see the wonder of the lifecycle of frogs. The once crystal-clear water turned a dark, murky green, and was laced with long chains of frog eggs.

With the influx of frogs, and my fascination for fairy tales and happy endings, I wondered, *if I kissed one of the toads, will he turn into a Prince?*

But then, there was also a probability that I might turn into a toad. I already felt like one. I giggled and immediately dropped the idea.

The invasion did not stop there. The unique features that made our pool so special gave the slimy interlopers access to our living room and bathrooms. They quickly took up residence throughout much of the house. I even came to believe they were stalking me. One day I was on the phone when a frog leaped from behind a curtain.

"Aaaaahhhh!" I screamed and jumped around like one of them.

Screaming became my response to every frog I encountered (the bathroom was a particularly dangerous place.) I came to think of the frogs as a biblical curse.

I was desperate for a solution to our frog problem. I thought I had found it when I learned our school biology class was going to dissect frogs. I figured experimentation was better than the frogs deserved, and I quickly offered them up without an iota of guilt.

"I know where we can get frogs," I suggested to my biology class one day as we needed frogs for our experiments. "You just have to come and get them yourself."

I took my class on a field trip to my house and hoped to end the curse of the frogs. I thought of my class as a frog disposal unit and hoped they would catch them all. However, the frogs had outbred the biology class's need for them. There were endless cables of frog eggs ready for hatching. The Frog Invasion was a reminder that the sting of our problem continued to haunt us.

I know the world is filled with real human tragedies; the loss of our pool was not of great magnitude. Yet, for young kids like us where our swimming pool transported us away from the harsh realities we faced, this proved to be a new misery we had to endure. At least today I can look back on the 'Great Frog Invasion' with a sense of humor and I'm grateful for the good memories.

13 HOPE

September 1975

Christmas songs blasted on the radio while torrents of rainwater splattered on the windowpane of my parent's room. The minute we reached the *'ber' months*, Mom would decorate the whole household with vibrant Christmas decorations, lights, and a Christmas tree that reached the ceiling. The Philippines always has had the longest Christmas season. But not this season; this was the time to forget!

I reached out to the picture frame of Dad and Mom on the nightstand and held it against my chest. It was their wedding anniversary photo taken right before Dad went to prison—Mom's smile etched on her cheek and Dad's twinkle in his eyes triggered a melancholic reaction. *I miss them so much.*

While Mom spent most of her time in Manila to be closer to Dad, we had a succession of caretakers in our home. Our 'governesses' were less than attentive to our needs, and with our rental guests, they were called upon to provide extra services. With our failing finances as a constant concern, Mom decided that our nearly empty, spacious home could easily accommodate boarders and augment the family income.

It started with occasional visitors and progressed to a steady stream of renters to occupy the empty rooms. Realizing her strategy was successful; Mom raised the stakes and decided to rent out the rooms to airline personnel, mainly stewardesses and pilots for their itinerant schedules. I felt awkward and scared to share our home with strangers, so I isolated myself in my bedroom, but loneliness was now my unwelcomed friend.

I set the picture frame aside and marched to the bathroom. Staring at the mirror, a bulge in my stomach screamed at me. *You need to lose weight.* I examined my bronze skin, then reached out for the soap, rubbing it against my body over and over again. *Damn!* I spent hours devouring women's magazines as if they were the Bible. I never saw anyone like me on the pages— chubby, with bronze skin from being under the sun, and a nose that would never be regal no matter how much her mother pinched it.

"*Tubo, tubo, tubo,*" Mom would often say, hoping against all odds that my nose bridge would still grow. At this very moment, I did miss her torments.

I followed one fad diet after another and ended each day by binging on an entire loaf of bread or any carbohydrates that would knock me out. Food allowed me to wallow in my sorrows. If my food craving wasn't enough to send me over the edge, the raging hormones that overtook my teenage body would.

In the Philippines, being defined as beautiful meant for a lady to have ivory, porcelain skin, an aristocratic nose with mixed Caucasian features, otherwise known as *Mestiza.* At fifteen years old, I was nowhere near in the same category compared to my peers who bragged about dates, first kisses, and sexual encounters. Was I too fat and ugly to be loved? Surely, I wasn't the only girl who felt like this?

One day, after the rain ceased, I made a beeline to the driveway. The sweet scent of freshly cut grass filled my lungs as a bus pulled over to drop the stewardesses. They scurried inside the house with loud voices like predators searching for their prey, oblivious to the privacy a teenage girl needed. This was a typical day in our household where buses coming in and out of our driveway to pick up the stewardesses or pilots and taxis for the other boarders who were coming or going. At night, the visitors' parked their cars on the side streets. Our house was like a train station with strangers extending to the friends, suitors, or extended family of the boarders.

But the attractive women groomed to be stewardesses gave me a glimpse inside their elite and glamorous lifestyle. In the era of the sixties and seventies, stewardesses of Philippines Airlines were chosen primarily for their physical attributes—tall, beautiful, and light-skinned. They were trained in cosmetics, posture, and poise. They learned to walk like models and how to speak with confidence. There was, an airline-sponsored 'finishing school' called Karilagan Modeling School that trained aspiring stewardesses, models, actresses, and beauty queens to walk, talk, and generally be poised. The stewardesses wore a combination of fashionably sexy, but still modest uniforms designed by *Pierre Cardin.*

All this glamour naturally brought new attention to our home. Men would park outside our house to catch a glimpse of the women in uniform as they traipsed from taxis to our door - the 'hotel' of the most beautiful women in Cebu and worked up the courage to be bold enough to ask the women out.

The stewardesses were friendly to me, amused by my *tomboy* demeanor. They greeted me with, "Hey, Kiddo, there's a bunch of snacks on the table."

Sometimes they would leave packages of airplane leftover food, which I considered a treat since Nang Elena, our *Yaya,* cooked the same old food almost every day. I could determine the route they flew by the snacks they left on the table, and I did not care how old or stale they were since they were exotic treats for a bored and lonely teenager.

I learned that many of the young stewardesses suffered from homesickness and deeply missed their families and boyfriends. They often cried and complained about the loneliness when they weren't partying—a favorite activity of our boarders.

Eileen, a pretty, tall, Caucasian-looking stewardess rose to fame in the Philippines when her plane heading to Mindanao was hijacked. The event was widely covered in TV and radio news reports, and she was recognized for her bravery and calm professional disposition in the face of attack. She became an overnight celebrity, received a promotion which meant she surpassed seniority ranks and lifetime employment by the airline despite been recently suspended for being slightly overweight.

And then there was Carol, yet another towering beauty with glowing dark skin—a feature ironically not favored by the airline industry. She fell in love with John, a towering *Mestizo* and family friend, which everyone mistook for a basketball player. Carol befriended Candy and me so that we could spy on John when she was off flying. In return, we received presents and treats from her exotic travels. I looked up to her like a big sister.

After the hustle and bustle subsided, I proceeded to the kitchen to check on what snacks the stewardesses brought for me.

Emmy, a stewardess that looked like a movie star, popped in and washed the stains of blood from her blouse.

"What happened to you?" I studied her.

Emmy pined for a lost lover and dabbled in witchcraft, hoping to win back her ex.

"I slashed myself with a knife and suck the blood I needed for a spell."

"Oh." I shrugged wondering if this was a normal strategy.

Moments later, the stewardesses pulled me aside to the hallway to share stories about Emmy.

"Did you know that almost all of the stewardesses were scared of her and left me to share a room with her?" Pinky, a boarder whispered.

I shook my head bewildered.

"I was scared to go to bed every night, lest she practices any Satanic rituals on me while I was sleeping."

I didn't know how to react and was craving for some airline snacks. They continued to gossip behind

Emma's back while I made a French exit. I seemed to be the shock absorber of all these lodgers who would confide to me about their unwanted pregnancies, or dead-end relationships with pilots, married men, drug dealers, and losers. I was a teenage girl who didn't need more drama in my life, but on the other hand, I also devoured the attention they gave me.

While skipping toward my bedroom, Charito, a charming, soft-spoken stewardess with delicate skin hollered out to me. "Come here."

Her bedroom consisted of a vanity table with an array of makeup and skin products.

Sitting beside her, I studied how she applied makeup, admiring her reflection in the mirror.

"You need to apply a base moisturizer on your face daily." Charito massaged her face in tiny circles with a moisturizing cream.

"Why?" I asked.

"Of course, to look beautiful silly." She opened her eyes wide. "For men, but more so for other women as well." She winked.

I applied the cream on my face, mimicking how Charito did it, wishing it would transform myself to look more like her.

"That's perfect, now you know what to do." She patted me on the shoulder then applied a foundation, blushed her cheeks, put on a striking eye shadow, and finished her regimen with a berry-colored lipstick.

Gazing at this woman compelled me to be like her—beautiful, bold, and confident.

"Oh, and I can't live without my eyeliner." A quick line on her eyelids transformed her almond eyes.

I gushed. "Wow! You look beautiful."

"Thank you." She smiled. "Now it's your turn."

"For real?" I beamed.

She nodded and swirled the chair to face her and applied my make-up.

I closed my eyes, all giddy, feeling like a princess ready to meet her prince charming for the first time.

"Ta da." Spiraling the chair so I can face the mirror, Charito's jaw dropped. "Wow! You look incredible."

I leaned forward to get a closer look at myself at the mirror yet didn't recognize the person staring back at me. The teenybopper tomboy had transformed into an alluring lady. My cheeks flushed and for the first time in my life, I understood beneath my skin what it felt to be beautiful.

14 PHOTOGRAPHS
AND MEMORIES

February 2010

Months after Dad's passing, I excavated Dad's drawers; the maze of the things he collected. I stumbled upon old photos and ones that jumped right out to me were our class pictures from grade school, which were taken every year. Friends and family had to identify me from the rest of my classmates since we all wore our school uniforms, and everyone wore the same generic smiles and compulsory poses. I spotted myself in an instance since no one else possessed the same lost dazed empty look. Holding the picture close to my chest, I sighed and was transported back to the 60s when we were kids.

Candy and I slipped into our white starched shirts with cute blue ribbons on our collars, and pleated navy-blue skirts, school uniforms with the aid of our helpers. We were always late for school because our hair had to be brushed thoroughly and Mom did not want us to leave without massaging our scalps with coconut oil or rubbing my skin blemishes with *Manteca de Cacao,* so the scars would fade. Mom treated us like her live dolls.

I set the photo aside and found another one of me in different school, which made me recall how different it was from my previous school.

I'd managed to convince my parents to allow me to leave my Catholic, all-girls school, St. Theresa's College and enroll in a new, public high school program started by the University of the Philippines.

I was just eleven years old then, going from the sixth to the seventh grade. I was desperate to get out of the Catholic school even though the new school I wanted to attend didn't offer seventh grade and was a public school – a feature that my parents found alarming. After all, they insisted, they'd made great efforts to send us to a prestigious private school. Status was particularly important to my parents.

But I had my case ready. The University of the Philippines (UP) was set to open a high school in Cebu, offering only the first two years of high school as a pilot project.

"I would be part of the founding class of UP, among the pioneers of an institution that carried with it a national reputation for excellence. Graduates were successful and influential, becoming leaders in business, politics, and the arts. University alumnae were known as influencers, movers, and shakers," I argued my case to my parents.

I rationalized that having a daughter among those distinguished graduates would appeal to my parents.

"But my cousins and many of my friends were planning to enroll there as well (*many* was an exaggeration since there were only a handful.)"

I embellished my argument further leaving out the fact that UP would be coeducational, knowing this would raise a whole new barrage of concerns.

My planned and logical case nudged my mother further into my court. She tried to lobby Dad on my behalf.

"*Sigue na*, maybe she's right," Mom said.

But Dad was firm in his objections. "No, absolutely not."

I then abandoned all negotiations and flew into a 'girl-tantrum' pleading my case through a shower of tears and uncontrollable sobs. Finally, and reluctantly, my father agreed to let me skip the seventh grade and enroll at UP for my first year of high school but with one caveat.

"Okay, you can go, but only on one condition," he said. "Your sister comes with you. You will have to look out for each other!"

Candy raised her voice from behind. "No! I am perfectly fine where I am, I don't want to change schools!"

Fortunately for her, she was two grades behind me and got to remain at St. Theresa's for another year before joining me at UP. I was thrilled and looked forward to leaving behind the nuns, the uniforms, and strict rules to experience freedom for the first time in my life. I'd also experienced my first taste of victory. It helped me to believe that if I really put my mind to something and wanted it enough, anything was possible.

That nippy afternoon, the teacher decided to hold our classes in the garden for a change. This was one of the reasons I loved my new school. We were not confined to classroom settings. Sometimes we held class outdoors, or wherever the mood took us. I was always interested in Social Studies more than any science classes especially when we delved into History or Anthropology.

"Magellan was the first person to circumnavigate the world," our teacher Ms. Alino said.

"Yes and no," I butted in and continued my litany. "Magellan did not make it back to Spain. He died in

Mactan Island. Remember *the Battle of Mactan*, where thousands of Lapu-Lapu's warriors attacked Magellan with his army of sixty-five men?"

The class opened their eyes wide.

"Magellan arrived with five ships here in Cebu, but only one ship made it back to Spain. Magellan's crew of sailors ventured in his name, actually in King Philipp of Spain's name. They were the first to circumnavigate the world. Pigafetta, their historian, chronicled this event and described in detail the battle when Magellan was killed." I declared with conviction.

"That's great, Mita. You sure were doing your research!" Ms. Alino praised me in front of everyone.

Ooohs and *aahs* erupted from the rest of the students.

My skin felt flushed and despite being, shy I was proud at the same time. Little by little, I built my confidence and was no longer afraid to speak.

In stark contrast to my St. Theresa's experience, we listened a lot and took notes. In UP, they always encouraged discussions and supported you to speak your mind. The inaugural classes were small; probably this was one of the reasons I shed off my shyness. We were in a class of fewer than 20 people half the size as it were in STC—the total school population was less than a hundred from all walks of life. We got to know one another as members of a family. Even the teachers knew each of us as an individual. I had new friends! The popular girls liked me—though I couldn't understand why.

Unlike St. Theresa's where most of the students came from wealthy families and had luxuries like cars and drivers to ferry them to and from school, UP had a mix of affluent families and students from more modest means who walked to school or took public transportation.

At UP, we were encouraged to speak our native dialect while at the private school we were fined if we were caught speaking Visayan instead of English. In fact, at UP we were expected to be fluent in our native dialect and *Tagalog,* the national language of the Philippines.

Of course, the co-educational makeup of the school was particularly appealing to me. I was quickly approaching adolescence, and my interest in boys was changing. Even though I had five brothers and hung out with lots of their friends, it was different to have a crush on someone and consequently another motivation to go to school.

I was incredibly happy in this school, that I already prepared my uniform and books, a day prior. I have also taken the initiative to do more research, study, and prepare myself for class the next day. At St. Theresa's, I was always late and the last to disembark in the car. In class, I was usually daydreaming and had our helpers do my homework.

Gone was the generic, starched uniform I had to wear at St. Theresa's. Although I favored it, other students were not as financially well off, it became a burden. They asked the administration at UP to adopt the policy of wearing uniforms. After some debate and a vote, the decision was made. We would have uniforms. However, the students were asked to take part in the design so that the uniforms would represent the school and us. We designed hip fashionable checkered skirts and white shirts to go with it. The men voted on wearing jeans and a simple light blue shirt. This great democratic act made me embrace my new school even more.

I discovered a new talent when Ms. Reyes, my English teacher at UP, encouraged me to write. I wrote about a shoelace and breathed some life into the common accessory.

Ms. Reyes picked out my writing among all the submissions and asked me to read it out loud. I was so embarrassed because I poured my heart out not thinking anyone would read it. My cheeks turned red, while I read my essay.

I was surprised that everyone stopped what he or she were doing and was compelled to listen to me. After the read-out, Ms. Reyes pulled me aside and encouraged me to continue writing. It was the first time someone noticed and acknowledged that I had a talent. I was so hungry for compliments that it was on that day that I decided I wanted to be a writer.

I wrote to escape my current reality; experience an alternative dimension and I did not want to go back. Like reading, writing transported me to another world. Each time I read books and did not like the endings, I would rewrite them in my head to my liking. Every time I went home to my empty house, I wrote to fill in the vacuum, even if I had nothing to write about, I would stare at the blank paper for hours. All these stories and characters lived inside my head, and they became my imaginary friends. I was obsessed with a *happily ever after ending* just like in the fairy tales.

I developed a fascination for fairy tales and would listen all day to records of Sleeping Beauty, Snow White, and the Seven Dwarfs, and Beauty and the Beast. I was entranced when a romantic Prince Charming solved all their problems. This was the only way out of my misery I thought. I was on a mission. I sought my Prince Charming to kiss all my troubles away.

For me, the experience in school had been like a beautiful dream until Dad was taken away and everything changed. Then, I went from being excited and optimistic to feeling ashamed. The friendships I'd made at school slipped away. I was an outcast. I felt like the heroine of The Scarlet Letter—stained and blemished. As a child, I blamed myself. I'd stare in the mirror at my dark face, my flat nose, my too-round features, and tiny eyes. I was ugly. No one could like me. My father was gone. Schoolmates and neighbors turned their backs on me. "I hate you. Hate, hate, hate you!" I'd shout at myself while I rejected my reflection, and what little self-esteem I'd had plummeted.

I don't even recall how I made it through high school. Enthusiasm for my new school and all it offered also vanished just like my father had. There was no one attending my ballet or organ recitals, or parent-teacher meetings, or karate tournaments; no one there at all cheering for me on that important day that I received my High School diploma.

I remember, I cried for hours, my hands crossed over on my vanity desk, leaning my forehead on my arms. Then I would take a blank sheet of paper and start drawing a world map of all the places I dreamt of visiting and had fallen asleep on my desk. Each time I lifted my head to face the mirror, I would see blackness and an apparition of my older self.

"Come," She would call out to me and take my hand as we entered the labyrinth inside the mirror as she guided me and gave me a glimpse of things to come. We were trekking all the places I'd marked on the map. I was a globe trotter, traipsing all over the world in a backpack, confident successful, beautiful, happy, spiritual, creative, blessed with a big family.

My reflection comforted me. "Don't worry honey, we got this. All these things shall pass. Stick to me and we'll go places."

I held on to her promise in the vision of the future she'd shared with me. I had hope and faith for a better and brighter tomorrow.

Morphing back to reality, I perused more of Dad's photos and found myself wearing a dress. I could still feel the sting from Dad's remark during that time.

With my heart pounding and Candy beside me, I asked Dad if I could attend a party, "Dad, Can I please go?" This wasn't the first time I asked for permission.

"Where are you going? Who will you be with? What time are you coming home?" He demanded.

No matter how clear my answers were, the result was always the same.

"No." His adamant look meant there was no room to negotiate.

Finally, after too much begging on my part, he laid down the law.

"I'll always say no," He explained. "You're still too young to attend parties. When you debut on your eighteenth birthday, you can do whatever you want."

"But how come my brothers can go out?" I cried.

At the age of twelve, eighteen seemed like a lifetime away. So, the opportunity to go to parties and stay out late made possible by having no parent in the house filled me with hope and anticipation. That small victory was short-lived. After my father's arrest, I was no longer invited to parties. Friends stopped talking to me. I was stigmatized and shunned.

"I don't care what your brothers do." Dad faced me. "The boys can take care of themselves."

But the same was not true for my sister and me.

"As for you girls," Dad addressed Candy and me. "When you get married, you'll have someone else to take care of you and I can have peace of mind."

This remark left a stigma in my future relationships because I was always looking for someone to take care of me, which was already a disaster at the onset of relationships. I did not even know I could take care of myself until I was left alone, and I had no choice but to sink or swim. At the same time, Filipino parents found it challenging to let go of their children, particularly their daughters. It was common to find three generations living in the family home with everyone sharing financial obligations and family values.

As females, our roles were clearly defined. Since I had a questioning and rebellious streak, I saw our parent-free environment as a moment of liberation. I recalled how we were not allowed to attend parties, even those held at our own home, while our brothers were free to party all night if they pleased. I imagined how much fun and freedom I'd have and the parties I'd attend. There would be no need to beg permission as I had in the past when my mother handed all authority over to my father. On the rare occasions that I got his attention, the response was consistent.

I returned all the photos and closed the drawer, overwhelmed by all the bittersweet memories.

15 LIFE WINS

March 1976

While Dad was in prison, we treasured Mom's presence each time she was around. Candy, Paul, and I would compete for a space in bed with her. To be fair, she put us in a regular rotation for the coveted spot and added two more beds to her spacious room so we could all be together in the absence of our dad.

I anxiously looked forward to her visits and peppered our governesses Nang Felisa with the same question repeatedly. "When is my mom coming back?"

"I don't know." Robotic answers became as predictable to me as my pestering must have been to them.

But I had an inkling of a feeling that Mom would arrive today as the house didn't have a speck of dust.

Moments later, a car pulled on the driveway and the doorbell rang. *Mom's home.*

Candy, Paul, and I rushed to greet her.

"Mom, you're here." I clung to her neck with force.

She let go of my arm and examined her dress. "Easy now, I don't want my outfit to be crumpled."

I pursed my lips. "I'm sorry, Mom."

Candy and Paul kissed Mom on the cheek then followed behind her toward the hallway and into her bedroom while Nang Felisa and the driver rolled her luggage.

Although my siblings and I knew that our financial life had drastically changed with items of value being sold and food no longer in great abundance, others thought of us as a wealthy family living in a grand house. Before Martial Law, Mom would plan five to seven-course meals with soup, appetizers, main dishes, and desserts. But with Dad's arrest, we could barely afford meat. Mom became creative and substituted vegetables for the mix of expensive beef and pork when traditional *lumpia* was prepared for us. She tried hard to maintain the status quo. On our birthdays, even when Mom was not around, she still managed to make sure we had a simple feast with fresh *lumpia*, e*mpanadas*, and *pancit* for which was believed to provide long life.

Mom possessed a creative and entrepreneurial spirit, and before Martial Law, she had established many small businesses to maintain our personal needs and interests. She owned a tailor shop, and thus, we had a personal tailor who made clothes for the whole family. She was also the proud owner of a beauty shop and had her beautician to style her hair and makeup, and a masseur who regularly came to the house. Finally, she maintained a tiny *sari-sari* convenience store around the corner from our home which she named "Paul's Corner" - after my youngest brother. Anytime we needed miscellaneous items like snacks and shampoo, we had it within reach.

My siblings and I didn't stop babbling and fighting for Mom's attention, but Mom was too busy to notice. Addressing Nang Felisa, she said, "Did you buy the *pasalubongs* I requested? I need to bring it to Manila."

Nang Felisa nodded. "*Oo*, Ma'am." She scurried to the kitchen and came back with the goodies.

Each time Mom came home, she flew into a frenzy of buying and preparing all the goods she wanted to ship to Manila for Dad's comfort. She was a force of nature. She bought green mangoes and *danggit*, a popular kind of dried fish and a Cebuano delicacy, along with other delicacies from the islands. She would tightly pack them in huge baskets for shipping. I wondered why Dad would need so much when he was still behind bars. Mom delivered a dose of reality.

"These are presents for the officials so that Dad will get released more quickly," she explained to us.

Paul pulled Candy and me in a corner and spoke in a hushed tone. "Mom is not being honest with us about the gifts."

I gasped and never anticipated these gifts would be associated with bribery or corruption. They were, as she said, simply gifts for officers of the army and their families who might help facilitate Dad's release.

We left Mom to settle in knowing that at five PM she would summon us to kneel and pray the rosary.

Her visits at home also included a great deal of time praying and performing the rituals of the Catholic Church. She had created a sacred corner in her room, complete with a large altar.

Moments later, we knelt together, my mother, sister Candy, brother Paul and me looking up at painted and gilded statues of Jesus and the Virgin Mary accompanied by a host of saints hovering over us illuminated by flickering candlelight.

I looked up at the Virgin Mary statue; her eyes were full of sadness. I imagined she was feeling sorry for me. *Are those real tears streaming from her eyes?* "Mom, why do we have to do this ritual? Are we being punished?"

"Hush now. Prayer is good for the soul." Mom made the sign of the cross and led the prayer.

The soft chorus of our voices echoed. "Hail Mary, full of Grace, The Lord is with thee. Blessed art thou among women…" I believe I recited enough Hail Mary's and Our Fathers for a lifetime.

During the recitation of prayers, my mind always wandered to the games I played with my neighbors or the latest TV show. While chanting the rosary, it seemed like we were summoning all our ancestors who looked after us. Sometimes I dozed off into a lucid dream state and suddenly I would see different faces on the altar, some I recognized in my dreams and some I don't. One of the faces that were familiar to me was that of my great grandmother, Maria, even if I do not know what she looked like. I just knew in my heart that she was because she frequently visited me in my dreams. I'd like to call her my fairy grandmother, my *Oma*.

Gazing at the candlelight, I drifted into a trance. A faded figure appeared before me. I froze, but as soon as I had a clearer vision of her kind and loving presence accentuated with thick long lashes and almond-shaped eyes, I sighed in relief. She swayed her long, silky ebony hair that complimented her round face and perky nose. Soothing warmth emanated from her sweet embrace.

"What do you want to do today?" She asked.

"Oma, I'd like to swim with the whales," I said.

"Your wish is my command." She waved her magic wand.

In an instant, we were both at the Pacific Ocean, swimming with the whales, turtles, dolphins, and even non-threatening sharks in harmony, having fun.

Did I spot a mermaid?

"Where would you like to go next?"

"Oma, I'd like to walk on the moon."

She whisked her magic wand again, transporting us to the moon. I was light as a feather as we were both floating in space enjoying the buoyancy. I scooped some pebbles as souvenirs, while she waited patiently absorbing my joy.

It was my happy place where I felt intense love, while she showered me with her light.

"Oma, I don't want to go back anymore. Can I stay with you here forever?" I laid my head on her chest as she wrapped her hands around me in a hug.

She kissed me on my forehead, "You are going to be okay. You still have a mission to fulfill and have a lot of work to do. I will see you soon. Everything is going to be all right. Promise me, you'll live your best life ever?"

It sounded more like a loaded command, than a request. But every night when I felt particularly sad, I would summon her in my dreams, and she came and whisked me away to the next big adventure. I'd wake up and the memory of my dreams vanquished. But she always left me an ethereal feeling of unconditional love.

The shadow faded and morphed back to the reality in front of the altar.

I felt guilty about my mind's itinerant flow. I didn't dare tell Mom what I experienced or saw. When my attention did drift back to the prayers, I tried to make up for my idle thoughts by fervently praying for Dad's release. Staring at the statue of Jesus with the blessed heart painted on his chest, I could feel his heart pounding. I beseeched him from my own heart as if he was a friend.

"Father in heaven, please, please release Dad from prison and bring my mother and father back home. I don't want to pray the rosary anymore. I want to go out and play or watch TV, anywhere but here bent on my knees. Thank you, Jesus!"

Along with Mom's nightly prayer ritual, I recalled her regular trips to the Carbon Market in the heart of downtown Cebu. There, with my sister and me in tow, she would seek out pawnshops and merchants who would give her the best deal on her jewelry and other treasures. The funds raised from these visits were used to purchase more gifts for guards and officials who were in positions to grant Dad some leniency or, ultimately, his release.

After reciting our prayers, I followed Mom like a lost puppy to her bedroom.

I perched myself at the edge of the bed, while Mom situated herself on the vanity table and applied some cream on her face.

"Mom, when are you going back to Manila?" I asked.

"Tomorrow," she said.

A jab punched me in the gut. "What? But you just arrived?

"Your father needs me."

I swallowed hard wanting to tell her that I needed her too, but instead, I asked, "When will you come back?"

"I don't know," was Mom's curt reply.

As Catholic children growing up in the Philippines, we didn't dare question the authority of our parents. I had no one to talk to, felt abandoned and frightened, and there was no way to express my fears, even as fate took our family to ever-darker places. Deep inside, I felt like a stray dog without a home.

After Dad's arrest, Mom followed his tradition of coming and going. She felt her place was in Manila, where she could attend to Dad's wellbeing, and only occasionally came home to check in on us. Gradually her visits to Cebu became even scarcer. I couldn't admit it then, but I now realize just how much I missed her daily presence.

I missed watching her nightly beauty ritual before she went to bed as she massaged her face in little circles. "Make sure you wash your face every night to minimize wrinkles," she'd tell me. Her fingers worked the Ponds Cream into her cheeks, forehead, and chin. I think today that her nightly beauty regimen worked magic – she had very few wrinkles, even as she was closing in on age seventy.

The next day, Mom was ready to board the car with all her luggage and boxes of gifts. As the driver was loading her baggage in the car, my eyes welled up and before she could see my tears, I immediately tug her arm, pulled her body next to mine, and wrapped her in a tight embrace, desperately clinging to her.

After feeling my heartbeat and absorbing my emotions, Mom disengaged abruptly. She needed to go.

"Nang Felisa, you'll oversee the children, okay?" Mom stammered between tears. "I trust that you'll take care of them as your own."

"Oh Ma'am, don't worry," Nang Felisa assured my mother, who could not have known how empty that promise was. The extent of her care and control over us was limited to putting food on the table and then shuffling off to her room. From the day my mother left to be near our father, my siblings and I were like wild weeds growing without the hand of an attentive gardener.

***

Once Mom was off to Manila and mostly absent from our life in Cebu, all those luxuries faded into the past. The businesses she supported suffered from neglect and no longer provided supplementary income for our family. The luxuries of life vanished almost overnight, including the fine clothes, the personal care, the bountiful meals, and even our place in the community.

All this was happening simultaneously with the inevitable trauma of adolescence. My sister and I were growing out of our clothes.

That Saturday morning, I asked Candy. "Hey sis, can I borrow your floral blouse?" I was getting tired of my clothes especially when I felt tightness at the waist.

"Sure, no problem so long as you loan me your red dress," she said.

"Deal." We high fived.

It didn't matter if the clothes were hers or mine since they always looked better on Candy. This made me irritable and annoyed that I reneged on our deal. I would hide my clothes and sometimes rip her nice dresses apart.

After Candy handed me the floral blouse, she asked, "Where's the red dress?"

My lips formed into a thin line. "I dunno'."

Dealing with the physical and emotional changes of a new stage in life meant staying indoors and feeling worse about my appearance. I remember how awkward and embarrassing it felt to tell my mom that I needed to purchase a bra. And when my first period arrived, I had no understanding of what was happening to my body. I thought that I was going to die.

So, in the middle of our argument, my sister called Mom long-distance and spilled the beans on me.

"Mom, Mita has been taking my clothes, but she won't lend me hers," Candy complained.

I grabbed the phone from my sister. "That's not true, Mom."

"She's just making it up."

"Please girls," Mom begged.

"You only have each other. For my sake, please don't fight anymore." To pacify us, she added. "Everything will be okay."

Mom was so trapped in her circumstances that she hadn't noticed my little sister and I were growing up, experiencing the accompanying mystifying physical and mental challenges of adolescence at the same time as we dealt with our family's trauma. I know now she was not to be blamed. With seven kids at various ages with a host of different needs and a husband who was a political prisoner, Mom had a lot to juggle. It was forgivable. It was understandable. But that understanding naturally evaded the mind of young teen, and her lack of attention only added to my suffering self-image and sense of isolation.

After we said goodbye to Mom, I scurried to the closet with Candy lagging behind me, pulled out the red dress, and threw it at her.

"Gee, I don't know why you're so angry, it's just a dress." She glared at me then barged out of the room.

Facing the mirror, I tried on the blouse Candy lent me then scrutinized my body and wept. *I can't stand myself.* I want to evaporate from this planet.

Along with the challenges of becoming a teenager, I was dealing with serious depression, though I could not recognize it at the time. I always felt guilty despite knowing that none of the tragic events in my life was my fault. Yet, I continued to blame myself. I wasn't smart and pretty enough. Everything in my life was out of control that I was exploring ideas on how to kill myself painlessly.

I spent days at the library and explored 1001 ways to kill myself without suffering. It got to the point that I got a blade to slash my wrist, seeking a visible vein, but then I stopped.

Nah, there must be another way.

One of the books, I read indicated that you ground glass into tiny particles and sprinkle it on your food. This would cut your intestines and you would bleed internally without being in any pain.

Is there a life after death?

I devoured books on angels and near-death experiences. I needed to know what happens after death. Not having the courage to cut my wrist or munch on glass splinters, maybe running away would be easier?

What happens next, where do I go from here? I hadn't worked a day in my life; I was accustomed to my parents providing for me.

I had a serious problem, and I needed an escape plan. I felt like I was in prison; I was trapped in these unusually strange circumstances.

How do I get out of it ?

I was desperate. Removing the blouse I borrowed from Candy, I slipped into my shorts and T-shirt and decided to use glass sprinkles to seal the deal. Heading to the kitchen, I noticed that our helper prepared *misua* soup that day, so I poured some in a bowl and proceeded back to my bedroom. I tore a piece of paper from my notebook, grabbed a pen, and scribbled.

Dear Mom and Dad,

I'm so sorry for doing this, but please don't blame yourself for what happened. Always remember that I love you both very much.

Your daughter,

Mita

Trudging to the bathroom, I locked the door then ground a coke bottle splinter on the marble countertop and added it to my soup.

Facing the mirror, I said, "Goodbye world!" *Will the world even notice that I am gone?*

Just when I was about to gulp the *misua* soup, a knock intruded my reverie.

"Mita, where's my black shorts? You said you would return it last time and I don't see in my closet." Candy continued to rap on the door.

"Leave me alone, Candy."

"I'm not going anywhere until you give me back my shorts," she persisted.

I stared at the *misua* soup. *Shit! What was I thinking?*

A loud thud roared in my chest. Tearing the letter into pieces, I flushed it down the toilet together with the *misua soup.*

Remnants of the paper floated in the water. I flushed the toilet over and over again until nothing was there.

Beads of sweat trickled down my neck. I opened the door. *Wow, that was a close call!*

"Finally!" Candy heaved a sigh.

I drew in a long breath and exhaled. *The gift of life won.*

16 FREEDOM CHIMES

July 1977

I graduated from High School at the age of sixteen and enrolled in De La Salle University in Manila. With Dad still in prison, it was a serious financial stretch to afford this university, but a quality of a college education for his children was a high priority for my dad. Against her wishes, Candy was also forced to move to Manila and enroll in a new high school. It was important to Dad that his daughters remain together. An additional benefit was that Jake was also in Manila for college. Rudy also moved to Manila to study Engineering in Mapua and was hoping to help Dad out in his business. However, his addictions interfered, and he quickly dropped out of school.

De La Salle University was the choice for the children of movers and shakers in the Philippine society. Even President Marcos sent his son to the university before transferring him abroad for further studies. Alumni of De La Salle included past and future mayors, governors, professionals, and entrepreneurs.

No doubt, as a businessman, Dad thought of our education as a good business investment.

That afternoon when I sat in my accounting class, I overheard everyone whispering amongst themselves.

"Harvey S. is in the class," Jinky, a classmate sitting beside me mumbled in a hushed tone.

I faced her direction examining who she was talking about. "Who is Harvey?"

"He's sitting at the back, please don't look!"

She glared at me. "Do you come from a different planet? Don't you recognize his family name?"

"They own all these megamalls all over the Philippines. They are one of the richest families in the country."

Indeed, the university was teeming with notables and children of extremely wealthy families. Once I even met a genuine star on campus but failed to recognize him. The famous actor who hosted a dance show every Friday was older, heavyset, and looking like an imitation of Elvis Presley with Elvis sideburns and posters of himself all over campus. He was disappointed that I didn't recognize him.

I brought my lack of self-worth with me to college, so this and so many similar encounters added to my feelings of being out of place in a rarified and elite atmosphere.

"Oh!" I mused that my education of who's who in the country was parallel to reconciling of my balance sheets. I focused back upon homework and patched up the numbers.

Jinky rolled her eyes.

The bell rang and I dashed outside toward the hallway to attend my next class.

An entourage of models was ambled in my direction. These glittering flashy *fashionistas* dolls with their fit bodies drew a commotion from other gawking students as they passed.

I paused briefly and merged with the crowd of admirers. "Wasn't she featured in the Sunday lifestyle magazine last weekend?" I asked, referring to the tallest lady in the crowd.

"Yes." One of the students from the crowd responded. "Isn't she beautiful?"

I proceeded to the locker room and grabbed my books.

"Hey *Chika*', I've been calling you all weekend." While tying her shoelace, Barbara, one of the tall, fair-skinned model, with jet black shoulder-length hair said to her companion who was a known designer with her own fashion line. "Where were you?"

While looking at her compact mirror, Sarah pursed her lips then applied lipstick and inspected all angles of her facial features. "I just got back from a shopping spree in Hong Kong."

From the corner of my eye, I could estimate how much she was worth by counting the designer labels she wore from head to toe. *Php 100,000 tops. Some people were just born lucky.*

I closed my locker and headed to my English class trying to feel like I was worth a million bucks despite my creative wardrobe choice being worth an estimated five hundred pesos.

"Cool colors!" Ruby, a college friend remarked as we brushed elbows on the way to class.

One thing for sure I could be proud of is developing an acquired taste from hanging out with the rich and the famous.

By then, I knew that Dad was struggling to raise the money for my tuition. This also meant that I didn't have the clothing allowance that would allow me to compete with the other smartly dressed students wearing brand names like Lacoste, Polo, Hang Ten, Gucci, Adidas, and other imported brands that implied the proper status. Nevertheless, I managed to be creative and pull together a wardrobe that proved at the very least to be presentable.

I hunted for bargains in the mall and would spend hours in front of the mirror appraising my appearance. I needed to lose ten pounds, pluck my eyebrows, and curling my hair in tresses with a hot iron to emulate Farah Fawcett's long feathered mane; Charlie's Angels was one of the most sought-after TV shows.

Nonetheless, my sister and I did continue to enjoy some vestiges of our formerly privileged life. My parents leased a roomy house in Manila for us. There was a maid for the house and a driver to shuttle us to the university. Dad discouraged us from working so that we could focus on our studies without distractions. I was positive that at the back of his mind, he hoped Candy and I would nab wealthy, influential husbands who could improve our family's faltering finances.

Being in Manila at this time also meant that we had an opportunity to visit Dad more often. He was in and out of prison for medical care and under escort he was able to drop by our house several times a month. Together with Mom, we also visited him at the clinic, which he considered a small family reunion. When Dad was moved to the medical unit of the Malacañang

Palace, Mom went the extra mile to visit the officials in another office to beg for Dad's early release.

After school, the driver picked up Candy and I and we met up with Mom outside the medical unit to visit Dad.

Upon arrival, a heavy tension filled the air while the soldiers barricaded the entrance. I caught a glimpse of the unit—spic and span. *What's going on here?*

"General Fabian Ver is in the clinic," The soldier advised us while inspecting our ID's.

The General, who happens to be the right-hand man and former Chief of Staff to President Marcos, made a rare appearance at the clinic.

It was now or never!

Mom pleaded with the officer to let her in. "I need to see my husband."

Hesitating, the officer opened the door ajar, and Mom inched her way in while Candy and I trailed behind her.

"It will only take a minute." Mom reassured the officer then stood before the tall, composed, regal General Ver, who flipped through the documents, the mountain of files on his desk.

Mom cleared her throat before she rehearsed her impassioned and tearful appeal for Dad's release.

Using General Ver's native dialect, *Ilokano*, Mom pleaded. "*Pakawanen nak kadi.* I'm so sorry to disturb you, General, we are here to request for your mercy, and if you can please release my husband. He has done nothing wrong."

General Ver shook our hands and pulled three chairs for us to join him at the table. "Please don't let your daughters see you cry." He seemed more concerned about our well-being. "Who is your husband?"

Hearing Mom's plea in *Ilokano* must have pierced through his hard-core exterior since he gave her his undivided attention. *The dialect was the key.*

She blew her nose. "Mateo Zara."

His eyes swept the ceiling like he was trying to find answers. Then facing Mom, he said, "I'm sorry, but your husband's release is not in my power."

Mom burst into tears while Candy and I consoled her.

General Ver rose from his seat and escorted us outside the office, and before bidding us goodbye, he added, "But I will see what I can do."

With shoulders slumped, nobody spoke as we stepped inside the car and rode back home. Feeling powerless and helpless like when Dad was stripped away from his family, I learned the art of being stoic so I could cover up the pain and shambles mutating like a cancer inside my heart.

***

The following weeks seemed like a blur to me, but I continued to focus on school and writing in my journal. I kept a straight face in front of everyone and as soon as I got home from school, I retreated into my bedroom and dove into my bed. Closing my eyes, I drew in a breath. My biggest fear was Dad might be too old when he gets out of prison.

A knock intruded my thoughts.

"Leave me alone, Candy."

The knock became louder.

Bolting upright, I rushed to open the door.

Standing in front of my very eyes was Dad in the flesh. I blinked twice. "Dad? For real?"

"Mita!" We locked in a tight embrace and tears lagged down my cheeks.

"Please don't cry, I'm home now." He studied me from head to toe. "You're so grown up. I missed you so much."

We hugged again and I didn't want to let go. "Dad, you're home. I can't believe it. I missed you too. Are you FREE for good?"

"Praise the Lord, yes!" Dad said.

I just can't believe it! Dad released? All our prayers were finally answered.

Dad experienced a gradual release before he was finally set free for good. Dad was given two to three days out of prison and just went back for formalities. He had a couple of soldiers who accompanied him, wherever he went. Dad took advantage of his partial freedom and visited construction sites, managed bank runs, and was even able to go for a brief visit to Cebu. This was possible if he took care of his security guards, which he heavily bribed with money and any other special favors he could swing. At the end of the day, he always reported back to Malacañang.

Dad's release happened so abruptly that I had no time to prepare for a party with welcome balloons and a little feast.

Dad relayed that he and his cousin Ralph were called to the Presidential Security Command Headquarters where Colonel Balboa declared them free men, but not before giving them some advice.

"You can go home now," The Colonel had said. "And it would be best if you no longer engage in any political affairs."

Dad recalled those simple words and the lack of formalities.

"I could not believe what I was hearing." Dad squeezed my arms. "There were no release papers, no documents, nothing. Nevertheless, I was so elated."

He was also suspicious, wondering if they would both be shot the minute, they turned their backs. "I didn't care," he told me. "I was just ready to go home."

The release came just in time. When Dad reached our home in Cebu, he found his savings depleted. "I had Php 3,000,000 pesos in savings before I was detained, which we lived on. And on the day, I was released, we were at the very end of our funds," he said. "I had to work immediately to catch up for the lost years."

It was the first joyous moment for our family in four and a half years. Wasting no time, Dad immediately flew back to Cebu, but since Candy and I were settled in Manila for school, we never again experienced the family life we had once taken for granted. And we found ourselves with some responsibilities we were ill equipped to handle.

***

While Dad was in Cebu, Candy, Jake, and I had moved to a Victorian house my dad had rented close to the University in Manila. He hoped it would help us be more responsible and bring some much-needed money into our diminished family coffers. We took in renters. I had no idea how to handle renters who were delinquent in payment. I asked my brother Jake to step in, but he refused.

We tossed up the responsibility among us. We were caught between pity and duty, and not one of us had the courage to put a reckless boarder out on the streets. Dad had major issues to deal with and left us to figure out how to be property managers.

I was worried about one tenant who occupied a room, named Arthur. He was skinny, tiny, wore thick glasses, and overall emitted a nerdy demeanor, while he buried himself with books. He barely left the room and looked every inch troubled. And to add insult to injury, he didn't pay the rent for several months, yet I didn't have the heart to throw him out on the streets. We just kept adopting strays who lived off our good graces. That was the demise of my landlord career.

It was challenging for Dad to revive his business especially when he did public works requiring that most of the paperwork go through the government.

The government employees were all Marcos allies, and they favored people who spoke their language. Consequently, he routinely lost the right to bid on government projects that had once helped to build the former wealth of our family.

Dad handled this dilemma by looking for work abroad, particularly in Guam and Brunei. With his lifetime of business experience and reputation, he acquired contracts and worked hard to rebuild the family's stature and finances. However, his new efforts never matched the life he'd built for us before the imposition of Martial Law and his years of imprisonment.

As in the past, Mom was often left alone in Cebu with her memories. Just as life had changed for Dad, without her children to hover over and care for, Mom's life also changed from a busy mother handling a bustling household to being a desperate wife supporting her imprisoned husband, to a woman (more or less) alone in a big house on an island. Seeking to be rescued, Mom turned to her faith.

The women in my family have a long tradition of religious belief. When the Catholic Church did not provide what my mother needed, she drifted further into a charismatic movement that was sweeping across our islands.

"Hey, Mom!" I had called her long-distance from Manila.

"How are you?"

"Praise the Lord!" was Mom's auto-response.

And if I had any questions or problems I needed to sort out.

"Call unto the Holy Spirit!"

With a cocoon of faith around herself, my mother became unreachable. She was unable and unwilling to deal with everyday life or even use everyday language. My questions were answered with biblical quotations that did little to comfort the restless spirit of a young woman.

"Honor your father and your mother, that your days may be long in the land that the Lord your God is giving you." She quoted the Bible verse when I was disobedient and resisted her orders.

When she grew increasingly frustrated and disappointed with my adolescent rebellion, or when the Bible didn't suffice, she took to *speaking in tongues*, a language that defied my understanding entirely.

"When are you coming home?" Mom asked.

"Next week, Mom," I said. "Why?"

"I have a weekly prayer group and would be great if you can join us," Mom said. "Bring your guitar with you."

I occasionally acquiesced, not because I sought conversion, but because the lead guitarist for the evening's music resembled the American blues-rock star named Johnny Winter, with similar long, flowing silver hair.

Our house now turned into a habitat of worship, as Mom gathered believers and devotees while they engaged in prayer meetings.

Before I knew it men and women sang praises to the Lord, while they danced, jumped, and bounced with their arms raised in the air. They concluded the session with *speaking in tongues* while others wailed and cried passionately praising the Lord in raw fervor. The highlight of the evening was the sumptuous snack and delicacies Mom invested in to draw a crowd.

"Why spare expense to a good and generous God?" Mom rationalized.

"Yes, Mom. I agree."

My father also claimed to have *found Christ* during his detention. Whatever Christian awakening he'd had was short-lived. On his many business trips abroad and around our islands, he returned to his previous practice of engaging in illicit affairs. Mom must have known as she retreated into her charismatic shelter, particularly since he used one of the church meetings to strike up a liaison with a member of her prayer group.

Life seemed to be at the point of no return. I felt out of place and abandoned. My goal was to run away, far away. As the years went by, I packed my bags and traveled from one country and continent to the next not sure what I was looking for but not looking back.

In retrospect, I realized my escape was due to never finding the little girl I used to be before Dad was taken away. The child who lost her youth, who could have and should have been happy, hopeful, and valued was pushed aside and left to fend for herself despite the incapacity to fathom and navigate adulthood.

17 DOWN MEMORY LANE

February 1975

The distance from my school to the house is a good twenty-minute walk. The driver is always scheduled to pick us up from school, but today I chose to walk home. Beads of moisture trickled down my nape. *Jeepney*s honked their horns as I crossed the street carrying my heavy knapsack. Oblivious to my surroundings, my pace slowed hesitating to go home to my bleak life.

Silence welcomed me upon arrival in the driveway. I slipped the key into the front door and stepped inside the house. *Where is everybody?* The stillness induced more gloom.

Proceeding to my bedroom, I changed into comfortable clothing then peeked inside the boy's room.

Nada. Where are my brothers?

Passing by Candy's room I confirmed that she wasn't there.

I headed toward the dining room, and no one was there either. Not even the helpers. *Where the heck is everyone? Our house is no longer a home!*

Before Dad's arrest, plates were always set on the table with rice, eggs, and *danggit* or leftovers in case anyone got hungry. But today, the only thing available was spam and stale rice. My stomach rumbled. *Emptiness, vacuum, lost in space... I used to have a family!*

I collapsed onto the chair my hunger dove deeper, screaming into the innermost chambers of my psyche. I plopped a slice of spam inside my mouth yearning for a dining table filled with jokes, stories, laughter, and with our complete family together savoring sumptuous meals. I missed the busy kitchen with diverse aromatic flavors that swept inside the house. The maids would wave their fly sticks to whisk off hovering flies and other insects while we ate. Mom had recipes for every dish that she'd organized in a scrapbook. My thoughts drifted to much happier times.

I thought about how our cook Esther would boil the *Bulalo*, while we hovered around her, enjoying the scent of our favorite dishes in the kitchen.

"Please be patient." Esther shoved us away from the kitchen.

Facing her eight-year-old nephew, Frankie, Esther instructed him. "Go to the store please and buy some Coke."

A meal was never complete without Coke, our Filipino red wine.

The very same kitchen and dining table that provided love, joy, and laughter was now abandoned and empty.

Not wanting to eat the leftovers, I set the plate aside and strolled toward the garden. Tall weeds, scattered leaves, and muddy soil greeted me like a contemporary friend. We did share one thing in common—we were neglected. I closed my eyes and could still hear Greg, the gardener's voice.

He'd have said, "Good morning, Ma'am." Greg, was a distant relative with a disheveled curly mass of hair with bronze skin and a pleasant smile, hailed me while trimming the lawn with huge scissors.

"Good morning, Ma'am," Alex, the governess' husband greeted me while scrubbing the tiles of the swimming pool.

The cleaning woman had a subordinate, there were several *yayas* available specifically assigned to take care of the younger kids like Candy, Paul, and me. Alex multitasked as a driver or gardener, and Felix, our main driver was always available to shuttle us around the island with an assortment of parked cars in the garage. There had always been people around.

Opening my eyes, climbing out of the chair, I strode to the house and entered the library that used to also be our study room. Mom was an educator before marrying Dad and reading was a priority for her. She made sure that we had comfortable lighting and chairs. She provided a soothing reading environment, to lure us into reading amidst a cozy and cool temperature so we wouldn't be distracted from the sweltering summer heat. This was our literary cave and our sanctuary.

Every time I asked Mom a question or how to spell a word, Mom sent us to the library with her most accommodating smile, to figure it out for ourselves. Our library was filled with dictionaries, encyclopedias and all kinds of classic books and novels. We were transported into a different world, wrapped in the captivating stories of Huckleberry Finn, tales of Robinson Crusoe, Moby Dick, Gulliver's Travels, and so many more.

I devoured fantasy, I loved worlds back in time, where it was safe to ride along with the new adventures from the pages of a book. If I wasn't caught in a violent storm struggling with whales in the middle of an ocean, I was shipwrecked in a remote distant island exploring my surroundings but determined to survive.

I enjoyed these stories so much that I was entertaining the thought of being a writer.

What me, a writer? No way! How did they do this? I believed writers had divine inspiration from the other side. Writing embers were ignited in my soul. This was my best-kept secret; I was going to be a writer.

Not wanting to linger anymore on memories, I shut the door of the library then paced back to my bedroom and daydreamed what it would feel if I met the teen beat idols, David Cassidy, Leif Garrett, or Susan Dey. With their posters hung on my wall, I religiously followed who they were and what they did. I channeled my boredom into their lives. I acted like most pre-teen girls and was fascinated by pop culture, U.S. movies, and rock stars.

I spotted my vintage guitar with a broken string in the corner. Tears spilled from my eyes and before I knew it, the Beatles song *'While My Guitar Gently Weeps'* played in my mind. I hummed the tune. *'I don't know how you were inverted. No one alerted you.'*

I caressed my worn and weary guitar and plucked its string, which made me recall my Uncle Bob next door who had a guitar-making cottage industry. He had encouraged his children and all of us cousins to befriend the guitar so we could learn to play it and practice some tunes. A popular chord book name Jingle Magazine was our daily creed.

Early on, Mom had noticed my affection for the instrument, which compelled her to order a custom-made guitar from my uncle. She also hired a guitar teacher for private lessons, and he started me off with a ukulele. My teacher loved singing songs and he taught me to jam with him on melodies so I could familiarize myself with the chords.

He never taught me any other styles like fingerpicking or slide; eventually I got bored with him especially when he was falling asleep while singing. In retaliation, I hid from him every time he'd come over, which caused him to give up on teaching me anyway.

In those days an American missionary family rented the house next door and Ursula, the missionary's wife taught piano. In an instant, Mom enrolled me in private lessons to keep me busy and entertained. Although I understood a few of the chords, Mom wasn't there to listen to the tunes I played. In the end, I lost interest in the piano too.

Mom did her very best to make me a well-rounded child engaging me in ballet, guitar, and piano lessons, all to keep me away from trouble and to provide me with all the opportunities she never had as a child. However, her good intention was, she lacked support;

Mom never listened to me play the instruments nor did she ever watch my dance recitals.

I wondered why I bothered when nobody seemed to care?

As a kid, I'd taught myself to play chess and table tennis and challenged everyone in the neighborhood. I was blessed to have relatives close by; we lived in a compound where cousins surrounded us. Although my aunt and uncle were not directly raising us, somehow, they kept an eye on us indirectly. I was at their home almost every day, and when they had their meals together, I came back to an empty home to eat alone. I did not know what my siblings were doing or their whereabouts. I presumed we were all busy surviving in our way. We disassociated ourselves from one another, each of us left to deal with our own pain and our lives.

A collection of tennis rackets and signature tennis shoes were displayed in one corner of my bedroom. During Dad's incarceration, two tennis courts were conveniently built across the street from our house and owned by a grand uncle. I woke up every morning to the rhythm of the tennis balls bouncing back and forth after the roosters' first crow.

With a tennis racket in one hand, I slipped into my tennis shoes and broke into a sprint toward the tennis court across the street. I found an old ball stuck in between the bushes, and it transported me back to my childhood playground.

With the tennis ball in my hand, I swerved my racket. The ball bounced to the other court where the players and spectators were. I used to sit in front of the tennis court with my grandpa, Tito Teofilo. He was my grandfather's brother. I never met my grandfather because he died too soon. My granduncle sat in front of the tennis court he built and was completely happy watching his sons play tennis and compete with other tennis players. When I sat beside him, he always spoke to me in Spanish so I could learn to speak the language.

I took to the game and played tennis at high noon when the temperatures and heat were at their peak, the sun scorching my skin. I had the court all to myself. I could play tennis to my heart's content without anyone waiting in line. Invariably, at the command of my mother, I'd hear one of the maids calling my name from our house. I'd run home and listen to my mom explain to me again, "You play tennis and swim only at night. It's not good for your skin!"

It wasn't the danger of skin cancer Mom was concerned about. It was the shade of my skin. In the Philippines, light skin represented beauty. Since I was a tone darker than my sister, who, like my mom, had porcelain skin and ebony hair, Mom thought that if she kept me indoors, and treated my skin with whiteners so that I might be marketable for marriage one day.

I admired the tennis greats, Chris Everts, Agassi Agassi, and Martina Navratilova. *Could I have been a tennis heroine?*

Still holding the tennis ball in my hand, already worn, peeled of its neon hair devoid of bounce, it was a painful reminder of yesterday and broken dreams.

Back inside the empty living room, old campaign pins bearing our family name. "Zara *kami*" propelled my thoughts to drift back again to when our home was a social and political hub when my father first ran for Congress in 1965. He'd poured out his heart and soul, exhausting his financial resources into that election campaign.

In those days, our house was bustling with people who included my entire family, helpers, security staff, friends, and relatives as well as extended family. Our kitchen staff was always busy, serving the outpour of people, food, and drinks.

Dad had launched a political jingle on the radio that chimed all over the island airwaves. It started with a whistle, then followed by the question in our Visayan dialect, *"Asa ka mu adto?"*

This prompted the response, "Zara *kami*!" This became Dad's campaign slogan. He printed the catchphrase on yellow T-shirts. (Yellow was his favorite color and symbolized hope.) We also distributed buttons, stickers, pins, hats, and other campaign paraphernalia bearing Dad's slogan until he became a household name.

Despite all his best efforts, he lost the election to Don Raymond Davide who was an established scion and a powerful political force in the region. He exerted influence over most of the town mayors in northern Cebu. Davide owned sugar mills, public schools, and cement-mill companies as well as gun industries. Davos City in the Northern region of Cebu was known as the 'Davide land.'

It was home to massive sugar plantations owned by tycoons who exported their sugar to the U.S., under the domination of Raymond Davide whose authority was unchallenged. As wealthy sugar barons, they ran the town in a godfather like setup. No one had the temerity to challenge his position for fear of their lives.

Dad's campaign had occupied all our time and energy for several intense months so many Christmases ago. Gift giving to many people at the holidays was a tradition, but the campaign caused our family's gifting list to explode. "*Pinaskuhan*, Ma'am!" was the common outcry of people we barely knew who flocked to our house demanding Christmas presents.

As the wife of a politician and candidate, Mom had had to be creative to meet the expectations of hordes of visitors to our home. Since so many families needed basics back then, she decided to buy yards of cloth as practical gifts. For men, she'd purchased a conservative pattern with neutral colors. For women, she'd selected colored or floral prints. We also handed out my father's yellow campaign T-shirts and even fed people who had come to our house. They lined up outside our home and waited for their turn; most being grateful but others complaining "*Gi-atay*!" which expressed disappointment they didn't receive more or better gifts.

By then the public already knew our house because we had owned a private water tank, which was uncommon in the neighborhood at that time. A few blocks away from our house was an impoverished *barrio* where they had no water. We woke up every day to a long line of our less fortunate neighbors carrying their buckets, waiting to tap water from our tank. We'd see them when we drove a car out of our garage. They would wave at us. "I felt like a little princess," my sister Candy remembers.

Strangers and extended family had also come to our house for financial support. *'Manoy, mangayo ko ug tabang,"* was their initial approach. They asked for money for medicine, births, deaths, and loans to help them through difficult times. Most claimed to be distant relatives.

I may have been disturbed by the constant parade of people begging, but my father had had a different perspective. "Just be content you are not the beggars, but the giver," he'd say, sharing his perspective and reminding us that, "Life is never equal. Some of you will be successful, and some of you will be poor. But you will not be poor forever, nor will you be rich forever. That's how the wheel of life works."

Staring at the campaign pin once more, I realized that everything we had was centered around family. Dad being the patriarch of the family had planted words of wisdom, but the minute he was taken away from us, our lives collapsed like a house of cards. We each had to pick up our own pieces before the larger puzzle could be completed.

18 MOM

You left before I could say goodbye
I don't know how or why,
I thought you would outlive us all
with your gracious generosity.

Now that you are gone,
I feel you much closer to me
and you have me doing the things,
exactly how you want them to be.

You did not give me a chance,
to say, 'I love you' to get to know you,
your life has been one big mystery.

All I have are memories of you,
a treasury of your journals and prayers,
imprints of the pious life you've led,
as the puzzle unravels.

So many questions remain unanswered
though bits and pieces have been falling in place
the picture gets clearer
as you visit me in my dreams.

Now I understand,
why goodbyes were not necessary
because YOU....
have never left me.

December 2012

With Mom gone and after Dad's death, my entire family were committed to each other to come home yearly during Christmas time, and granted our financial situation would allow it, to break the habit of having a family reunion during funerals. Together we dealt with matters whether they were complex or minuscule. Our issues consisted of whether to sell or keep the house, decorate our home for Christmas, or whether to support our half-brother, whose DNA we still questioned.

During this holiday, we addressed the season's urgent needs and decided on the bare minimum Christmas tree with ornaments and gifts mostly for just the kids.

While attaching the huge star above our Christmas tree, a jab penetrated my heart. A faint tune from Mom's dilapidated piano surfaced and led me back to a time when Mom was still alive, recalling all the Christmas holidays we spent together. The whole family sang Christmas carols while in a frenzy we packed gifts for a house flooded with well-wishers. *God, how I miss Mom.*

Although as children my sister and I were never allowed to attend the numerous parties hosted by our parents, especially during the holiday season, we witnessed the grand and opulent preparations. Then, Casino Español, an elite membership club with a gourmet restaurant noted for their delectable Spanish cuisine, catered our food.

My favorite dish was *Callos*, a stewed tripe dish, simmered for hours over low heat, a Spanish cuisine associated with the city of Madrid. We have our Filipino version, which is equally delicious. I also enjoyed nibbling on *Boquerones*, fresh anchovies marinated in vinegar or olive oil, seasoned with garlic and parsley best guzzled with Spanish white wine which is another popular appetizer found in Spain. Waiters in uniforms would dress the tables; they staged the house and brought in silverware and elegant dishes. Members of a popular boy band arrived to serenade the guests. A steady stream of known government officials walked in, accompanied by beauty pageant candidates and movie starlets stalked by the paparazzi.

The newspapers would broadcast the parties my parents hosted. One of the headlines read, "Romeo Vasquez graced the Zara residence with Divina Valencia," referring to a famous movie heartthrob visiting with his leading lady. I envied the ability of our brothers to attend these grand affairs while Candy and I were banished to our bedrooms. *How long did they want to preserve our innocence?*

We were pampered in many other ways. My mother not only had a personal seamstress who made clothes for her as well as for the entire family, she had her tailor store; a shop that specialized in sewing uniforms for the students that was strategically located in front of the school.

The leftover material from Mom's clothes was used to make matching outfits for my sister and me. This ritual started right before Christmas to ensure we'd all be similarly costumed for the season's festivities. My sister and I eagerly anticipated this time of year for the fashionable new clothes as well as all the bountiful gifts that Christmas promised.

One of those gifts was my father's presence. He often traveled on business, and we'd go for many weeks without seeing him. However, at Christmas, he made a point of being home with us. We'd wear our new matching outfits to fit the occasion. Like us, every inch of our spacious house was decked out in Christmas finery, while holiday music piped through the rooms. On Christmas Eve we gathered in the living room while Mom sat down at the piano and played familiar carols that we sang with joy until the clock struck midnight when we'd all amble off to church together to celebrate Midnight Mass.

But the night was not over. After Mass, we'd hop from one family's *Midnight Offerings* or *Noche Buenas*, to another. We ate specially baked hams and traditional

Christmas cheese called, *Queso de Bola*, and old-style midnight snacks at the homes of our relatives. Throughout Cebu, when the clock struck midnight on Christmas Eve, every door was open to welcome guests and celebrate the blessings.

Somehow, it is the beauty and abundance of the past Christmases that represent our family life before the imposition of Martial Law. Despite all our flaws, my dislike of school, the little spats I had with my siblings, and Dad's strict rules for girls, we were a whole family with a wonderful home that was blessed with abundance that we shared with others.

I remember those holidays fondly, in part because I could count on Dad being home. Since he operated a construction company, he was frequently gone to facilitate projects on other islands. We only saw him a handful of days throughout the year outside of Christmas. I was jealous of my cousins next door, whose father Tito Bob was always there for them.

"When is Dad coming home?" I'd pester my mom.

"Don't ask so many questions!" She would fire back. "He's working!" She would tell me to save up my questions for when he came home.

But even those uncertain holidays were a blessing compared to those we spent without him (and often

Mom after the arrest). With just one knock on our door, it was all gone—the decorations, the music, the traditions, anticipation, and joy.

I remember one Christmas after the arrest when Mom did come home. Instead of bringing warmth and familiarity to the holiday, it brought only more sadness. We were no longer invited to the parties and festivities that usually came with the season. Our house no longer had the spark and glitter that the celebration brought.

"Mom, should we decorate the house together?" We were fast approaching the month of November and our house appeared to be bleak and gray.

Before Dad's arrest, Mom brought out the Christmas décor to furnish the house in early October.

In response to my question, Mom just flashed her signature *Mona Lisa* smile. It did not dawn to me that Mom did not possess the Christmas spirit, or even the resources for festive ornamentation. No Christmas décor for this year. No huge packages of *haute couture* to wear on Christmas Eve. The only reminder for me was when Mom sat down at her piano.

She played Christmas carols like she always had. We would sing to our hearts' content and belt out our favorite Christmas hit list.

But after Dad's arrest, even the keys of the notes sounded slightly flat. We sang the words to familiar songs, but they took on a different meaning under the new circumstances of our lives.

"On the first day of Christmas, my true love gave to me."

And by the 7th Day of Christmas, tears spilled from Mom's eyes, and she could no longer play the piano. We all wept and spent Christmas Eve down on our knees, praying the rosary in the hope for Dad's early release.

But I learned more things about Mom after Dad was gone. She often seemed angry and very touchy when it came to questions about Dad, and I had faint recollections as to why she reacted that way.

"Mom, are you okay?" I'd ask.

"Just remember when you are married, you will not always be together!" Mom snapped.

"Huh? What do you mean, Mom?"

"Remember, when you were five years old, and we went to Davao?" Mom said.

I remembered the incident vaguely; I thought it was a dream.

"We boarded a plane to Davao which is an hour South of Cebu," Mom reminded me.

"I confronted your father and his mistress and told him that he had children at home who still needed him."

I did not understand the situation until I was almost an adult and learned more about Dad's extra-marital affairs, it explained his long and frequent absences from home, and accounted for Mom's lingering sadness.

Though I was too young to know that many affluent men in our culture had mistresses, my mom was surely aware of such poorly kept secrets! Perhaps that the anger she often expressed toward my siblings, and I was rooted in the hurt she felt over Dad's betrayal.

During our last Christmas gathering, Mom and I had a heated exchange over something trivial and before I knew it, Mom erupted like a dormant volcano. Whenever I'd do something wrong, Mom exploded with pent-up rage, well beyond what my small transgressions merited.

She seized a belt, or a clothes hanger, or whatever she could get hold of and whip me like a frenzied demon. I remember clinging to a curtain, crying not knowing what I'd done wrong. *Well, I admit being mischievous, but I didn't know for which thing I got the beating?*

The ordeal would last about a good hour, though it seemed like forever to me, and she would break down and cry afterwards. In between tears, she confided how my father had grown up on the streets and suffered as a child.

Huh, what does that got to do with my punishment?

She expressed her unconditional love for him. It was during these moments of grief that she'd hint at her upbringing.

"You are blessed," she'd say, "I had a terrible childhood."

For some reason, growing up, I thought my mom hated me and it was only I who got beatings until I bonded with my sister later in life; on one of our drinking sprees and she'd spilled the beans.

"Oh my God, did she do that to you too?" Candy asked. "Same here," she said. "Mom snapped and beat the hell out of me, I thought she'd kill me right there and then, only because I refused to dance for Dad and his guests at one of our parties."

It was strange that she did not raise a hand to the men in our family. Were they superior to my sister and I? Or were there things we were not aware of?

Many years later, four of my mom's sisters visited me in Cebu, and they filled in some blank pages. We hired a van, while we drove to the countryside, me being their tour guide. I took the opportunity to dig.

"Auntie Layla, Mom never talked about her childhood," I said. "Why is that? All I know is that she constantly repeats that she had an incredibly miserable childhood."

"Honestly, we don't know," Auntie Layla said, looking every inch like my mom's clone.

"We did not even know that we had four older siblings. One day, Mom took us to visit our Aunt Lucena, and voila, it was shocking to discover this."

I learned that she and her siblings had been separated from their birth family while very young. Her unmarried Aunt Lucena, who owned agricultural land, a farming business, and had sufficient financial resources, adopted them. Although Mom escaped the poverty of her birth parents in her new home, she also became a child laborer, working in the rice fields for her aunt's business. In that era, it was not uncommon for children to work alongside their parents. There was no such thing as *child labor laws* during in those days. Everyone, young and old, were expected to help for the survival of the family.

Perhaps this separation contributed to her rage and sorrow as our family went through the intense trials of my dad's infidelities as well as his detention throughout the years of Martial Law.

The fact that Mom came from such a difficult childhood to marry Dad and create the comfortable life our family enjoyed is testimony to the strength of her spirit. Our grand home in Cebu, the prominence of our family, the security and freedom we knew as young children was a gift that we just took for granted until it slipped away.

Mom was loved by her community, and I can't deny the pressure I felt to compete with her popularity. In my eyes Mom may have been a hero, but was also a martyr, and I dreaded inheriting that trait. As the oldest daughter, I absorbed her pain and it was SO much easier to smoke, drink, swear and be the *black sheep* of the family. I defied all the laws and traditions, as I paved my path onto this earth. Jaded by pain already, marriage seemed like a far-fetched idea. At one point, I believed that a mistress was treated better than a wife. I wanted to learn the rules, so I could purposefully break them.

I also suspected that absorbing Mom's anguish, it would greatly affect my relationships with men. I had very little patience and tolerance because I did not want to suffer and be a martyr like my mom who loved Dad unconditionally despite all his shortcomings. As adults, we used to tease her. "Mom, Dad is your bottle," referring to an alcoholic's addiction to the bottle. So, when a good thing got going for me, I'd sabotage it unconsciously, feeling that I didn't deserve a loving healthy relationship.

By that December in 2012, melancholy hit me as I gazed at the Christmas tree now filled with ornaments, and I acknowledged that we would no longer be spending Christmas with Mom and Dad who are both in heaven. Yet I still believe they are like the stars watching us from above.

19 LOVE

"I wanna' know what love is,

I want you to show me.

I want to feel what love is.

I know you can show me. "

- Foreigner, 1999

This may sound clichéd, but my quest for love is summarized in this stanza from the popular song of a British-American Rock band named, Foreigner.

Still dazed from Dad's funeral and going through the boxes, I opened one last box where he stored some more old photos. A faded, dusty, black and white photo of my parents stood out. *They looked so happy.*

Mom's words ingrained in my brain haunted me. "Remember, when you're married, it doesn't mean you'll always be together." Although Mom was the most faithful wife on earth, and she meant well injecting doses of her reality early into my system that allowed me to understand the context of her advice about her marriage. When I was younger, I was lucky to see Dad once or twice a year. He was almost like a mythical figure to me, and I believed back then that this was normal.

What this taught me is that love is the greatest thing of all, no book is rife without romance, puppy love, true love, or *Agape* love. I don't feel comfortable revisiting this phase in my past; I shun thinking of the pain I inflicted on others and likewise, the agony it caused me. I look back to the sweet, happy, and troubling moments in my life and I realized that they fortified my strength and spirit. I acknowledge that I had to walk through the flames of fire, to be humbled and made grateful. This journey brought serenity, humility, and self-love. The latter, I believe is the greatest love of all.

When I was younger, my exposure to men was limited to my dad's disciplinary restrictions, and to my brothers and cousins. I was fortunate to have many brothers who'd entertained their friends at home. While approaching adolescence with raging hormones, and being drawn to the opposite sex, the objects of my fancies, never knew I existed and were attracted to my better-looking older fair-skinned cousins.

Although online dating is the new norm in this era, the Internet didn't exist during the 60s. We communicated via chunky phones or when we'd accidentally run into a party-line—a local hardline telephone circuit that is shared by multiple telephone service subscribers. Occasionally, the phone lines would mess up and we'd end up making friends with other subscribers, which sparked friendships.

I put the picture inside my purse, wishing to linger in that memory of happier times. Sorting out more photos brought bittersweet memories. One picture compelled me to look twice—Rudy and his friends.

I held the photo close to my chest, missing his mischievous smile. *Gone too soon!*

The next photo caused me to squint. *Oh my God, is this Harry? Who can forget one's, first love?*

My thoughts drifted to Harry, the object of my fancy at the ripe age of fourteen. He was a fair-skinned kid, with voluminous curly hair, beautiful eyes, and thick lashes; he was tall and lanky with strong Hispanic features. The best part was he was one of my older brother's best friends, which was a bonus for me to see him. He always found an excuse to visit my brother and each time he was around, my heartbeat faster and made me blush. Our relationship started as phone pals, and we burned up the phone lines every night talking about everything under the sun and sweet nothings as well. When we finally got together in person, it was confirmed, he was my boyfriend and I was his girlfriend, whatever that meant at that time.

Since we were both incredibly young and Harry was also my brother's friend, we decided to go steady under wraps. This meant engaging in long conversations all night long but acting like distant strangers when we met in person.

Harry was extraordinarily thoughtful; he'd call me night and day just to say, "good morning" or "good night."

When Harry could afford it, which was quite rare since he was a struggling student still living with his parents, he'd buy me flowers. Usually, he plucked roses from his mom's prized garden and never came to visit me empty-handed.

"Oh, I got something for you."

"Goodness, thank you!" I received a bundle of roses with a peck on my cheek.

After being phone pals for a year, we agreed to date. Harry was too young to drive at fifteen years old, but he was able to wrangle a car from his parents. When he drove me to places where I needed to go, he never failed to open the door for me. *A gentleman indeed!*

Since our relationship was still a secret and being both movie *aficionados*, we decided to watch a movie.

I was nervous as we entered the dark chambers of the movie house. Harry took my hand and guided me to our seat. Despite the air conditioner in full blast, I broke into a sweat fearing someone I knew might spot us.

Harry was just as innocent as I was; he'd probably never been alone with a girl. He held my hand in a tight grip whereas; everyone else in the cinema house in our area was getting comfortable and heaving in pleasure with soft moans.

Harry and I looked at each other and did not understand what they were doing. We only had one date and all we did was hold hands the entire time while everyone else around us was necking and petting in the dark corners. I wanted to kiss but being so young, I did not know how.

A couple of months later, his family migrated to Canada, and I never heard from him again. I could not believe that the guy I was in love with also liked me in return. Since I was a pretty needy person, I probably would have fallen in love with any guy who paid a tad of attention to me, but I never forgot my first love and how he made me feel. Harry was my first innocent puppy love and the secrecy of it made the fruit that much sweeter.

Morphing back to present times, I kissed his photo then tucked it away.

I continued exploring Dad's photo box and I ran into my high school yearbook.

"Ha choo!" I sneezed wiping off the dust before opening the pages. *High School was not kind to me.*

In high school, though I hung around with the popular girls, while everyone was getting asked out for dates, I was the ugly duckling who was left behind.

I was transported back to when I was a student and my high school peers relayed their experiences of their first dates and the special night when they lost their virginity.

"Awwww, it was so painful," One of my peers, recounted her first night.

"And a lot of blood." They shared.

"Eventually, you'll enjoy it after overcoming the pain," they giggled.

But my High School years became the dark medieval age of my life when Dad was in prison and Mom had gone to be with Dad. I waded through life like a sore thumb, or an open wound.

I brushed my thoughts aside and rummaged through more photos in Dad's box. I stumbled into a picture of Noel and me.

Oh Noel, noel, my second love! My heart ached from the love that never transpired.

At sixteen years old, I moved to Manila for college and frequented the library for quiet study. This was the only place that was serene, and I could focus on my studies, but most of all, this is where I would catch a glimpse of Noel.

Oh my God, he's cute!

He was skinny, with long, silky jet-black hair and fair skin; he wandered along the corridors and caught my eye. My cheeks flushed and I pretended not to see him, but I stole glances while I buried myself in my books. This went on for a week or two and I could anticipate his coming and going. He must have noticed me too. I wished and prayed to find an opportunity to get to know him, but *nada.*

Then one day, I did not see him come to the library and my heart deflated like a balloon. Days dragged into weeks, and I was sick with worry and longing for a stranger I barely knew. I continued to visit the library and just when I decided to forget about him Noel popped in and sat right next to me.

"Hi, I am Noel Tumulak. I have seen you here frequently. What are you studying?" He asked.

Oh, my goodness! I can't believe he is back and talking to me. "Mmmmm… nothing." I shot him a coy look. *Dumb answer, what was I thinking?* I was tongue-tied, and I think he knew he had me at 'hello'.

"Can I invite you for coffee?" Noel asked.

YES!!! Without batting an eyelash, I said, "Sure."

I trailed behind him to the college cafeteria and settled in the corner table while Noel lined up to get us some coffee. His almond-shaped piercing eyes penetrated my soul.

Joining me at the table, he asked. "So what course are you studying?"

"Asian Studies." I tucked a strand of hair behind my ears. "What about you?"

"I am studying to be a Chemical engineer." He took a sip of his coffee.

"Your family name sounds familiar. Are you related to Senator Tumulak?"

He grinned. "Yes, he's my uncle… my father's brother."

I flashed him my heart-stopping smile, confident that my parents would approve of this young man even if his famous uncle belonged to the opposing party; he had the right network of connections, and his family was a product of Ivy League educations. Noel came from a decent family, who lived in the right zip code, and had all the credentials that would pass my parent's criteria for a perfect son-in-law.

Noel shot me a question. "Have you found Christ in your life?"

Weird question!

Before I knew it, Noel pulled out a booklet from his backpack and shared about Jesus Christ. "I used to dapple in witchcraft. I could not even go to church. Every time, I went to church a spike of nails stabbed on my spine and I'd break out in a cold sweat. Until one of my teachers introduced Jesus in my life," he testified.

My eyes opened wide.

"I would like to invite you to accept Jesus too as your Lord and Savior. He is the only way for your salvation," he said.

Like an answer to Mom's prayers, Noel brought Christ back to my life. After being dragged to daily rosary rituals, prayer meetings, church services, and convents, I abstained from God and religious activities whenever I could.

Noel was an active member of the "Campus Crusade for Christ" and revived my faith bringing it back into my life.

I nodded. *Yes, I'd go to the ends of the earth with you.*

After the brief coffee interlude, we were inseparable.

The first time we got intimate, I was in a state of shock that men's private parts were different from a woman. *Why didn't anyone tell me? How could I have not known males were anatomically structured SO differently from women, though I had brothers I'd never seen a naked man before?*

I quickly recuperated from my surprise and pretended everything was normal and we made love and slipped into each other like we had known each other for many lifetimes. I was in a state of bliss. I was whole and one with him; I saw our children and great-grandchildren in his eyes. I looked up to him lovingly and noticed that Noel was tense, grim, and his facial muscles tightened into a frown. I was confused.

"You said I was your first?" He darted a nasty stare.

"Yes, I have never been with anyone before." *But where were the pain and the blood that my friends spoke about?*

When we made love, it was the most beautiful natural thing in the world to me. So, I wondered how I broke my hymen? Riding a bike perhaps? I loved biking and was a proud skillful biker, riding around in circles without my arms touching the handles. This issue was a grave concern for me. My honor depended on it.

Despite the disastrous first night, we continued to go *steady*. The plan was for Noel to finish his studies and we would get married. He did not formally propose to me, but I just took it for granted that we would be together forever. Noel was in his last year in college, wanted to wrap it up, migrate to the US, and somehow along the way he'd marry me. So, when I informed him that I wanted to take a break and visit my hometown on Cebu for the summer, he was relieved.

His final year in college was challenging and he needed to focus on his studies. I guess fate had other plans for us, because once I got back to Cebu, I took a summer job at Cathay Pacific airlines; I enjoyed my independence and earning my keep compelled me to stay. Noel came to visit me and at that moment, I knew he wasn't the one for me. We broke up and moved on with our lives.

I set Noel's photo aside, wondering what would have happened if we'd ended up together?

As I continued to unearth pictures, I spotted Kalle's photo facing the ocean, with his hair being swept by the wind.

I read what was inscribed at the back of the picture. *If you do not understand my silence, you will not understand my words.*

A teardrop. I thought Noel was my *true* love until I met Kalle.

If there is one word, I could describe my relationship with Kalle, it was *crazy*! I fell in love with his madness.

It was one boring summer when I worked at the ticketing office for Cathay Pacific and Northwest Airlines. At seventeen years old, this was my first real job aside from my stints at my father's office. After a full day of taking phone calls, filing, and issuing tickets, I could not wait for five PM so I could clock out. Five minutes before we were about to close the office, a towering man with thick blonde hair who resembled Clint Eastwood popped in. I was awestruck and didn't even notice his companion.

Oh no! I was ready to go home but my boss implemented a *customer-first* policy, and I had no choice but to let them in. "How can I help you both?"

"I'm Kalle and this is my business partner Jared." They both gave me a tight handshake grip.

"I'm Mita. By the way, do you run?" I blurted out, my eyes never leaving his.

He winked. "Yes, I am a runner, how did you know?"

At that moment, I knew we'd be together. I could spot a runner a mile away. A runner for me was someone who didn't just exercise, but a person running away from trouble, from their realities, or from themselves. I could smell them, and I'd be magnetically drawn to them. They resembled a big part of me. Later on, I learned that Kalle was indeed a runner; his father was a retired military man. He woke him up at five AM every morning since he was a child of five years of age to run in the forests of Bavaria, in rain, snow, or shine. Kalle was also running away from a rigid strict disciplinary Catholic family orientation. What's not there to like about him?

Kalle and his business partner needed help to sort out their plane ticket to Europe. I assisted them; working on their itineraries and at the end of the day Kalle had asked for my home number. I had never been with a foreigner before and my only brush with foreigners was when my family hosted an exchange student one summer from the US, but when Kalle and I started dating, I was surprised with the range of independence he allotted me. When we attended parties, he liked to mingle and shine with his stories of adventures. At first, I felt weird because I was used to clingy Filipino relationships where we hang on to each other.

I confronted Kalle, "Why did you drag me to a party and leave me as soon as we arrived?"

"But we are together all the time, aren't we going to parties to mingle with people?" He reasoned out.

I was an insecure teenager and intimidated by people who were judging and appraising me from head to toe trying to figure out what was I? *Am I a hooker, a mail-order bride, or something in between?* When they heard my surname was 'Zara', they acknowledged that I came from a good family. I never had to deal with this when I was with a Filipino boyfriend.

As our relationship blossomed, my parents were upset because he was moving around my family's circle and heard unfavorable stories about, he and Jared, the society's elite columnist. Cebu after all is still a small town but Kalle was aware of this. To dissipate their fears, he invited my parents for dinner to assure them of his noble intentions, but the dinner ended up a disaster.

We went to the Beehive restaurant where they had good steaks and a notable variety of European food.

As we ordered food, perhaps Kalle felt a need to share more about himself, so he blurted out, "I rode on a bike from Germany to Africa."

"Really?" Dad and Mom kept a straight face.

"I also hitchhiked all over the USA," Kalle continued.

My parents eyed him like he was a bum.

Not wanting to read my parent's mind, I cut my steak, mincing it in a thousand pieces anticipating an explosion.

Not being able to contain himself, Kalle cleared his throat. "I would like to ask your permission if I may take Mita on a vacation for a month or two. We would like to travel North on a motorbike."

Dad coughed and spat out a piece of meat. "Excuse me?" He turned toward my direction with a look of horror in his eyes.

Mom pacified him and took a huge gulp of water.

I believed my parents assumed that he would ask my hand in marriage and make a decent woman out of me, but it was far from Kalle's agenda.

Kalle seemed not to understand my father's reaction; he thought he was being respectful and honorable by asking their permission!

A knife fell from the table. It was a sign. *Time to leave.*

After the awkward goodbyes, the ride home with my parents added more pressure.

"You can't see this guy any longer," Dad commanded.

"It's all fun and games for him; this man is a bum!" Mom chimed in.

My parents especially my father was insulted and disgraced by his behavior. They gave me an ultimatum to stop seeing him or else. The inner rebel in me flourished, especially when under pressure. To my parent's disappointment, I packed my bags and left.

Kalle and I leased a flat in the city and also built a native house in the mountains. Living in a native cottage up in the mountains was mutually exotic for both of us. Since Kalle was an academic before his adventures, education was important for both of us. I wrapped up my degree in History at the university while he worked during the day, selling diamonds and jewelry with his partner, Jared. In his spare time, Kalle taught me German and indoctrinated me with the literature and history of Germany in the event we would move there in the future. At the end of the day, after Kalle came home from work, he couldn't wait to get rid of his suit, put on his rags, and off we went to the mountains or the sea on his motorbike.

During holiday breaks from school, we toured all over the Northern Philippines as well as the Southern Philippines in his motorbike. He took pictures while I wrote travelogues and submitted them to the local newspaper. With my penchant for history and writing combined with his photos, I was able to produce articles that were sometimes featured on the front page of the local newspaper. I had no idea that my mother was following trips and had created a scrapbook of my articles. The last time she did that, she created a scrapbook on Apollo 11 when they launched the rocket to the moon.

My parents had resigned themselves to the fact that I was a lost cause... more like a rebel without a cause. Mom continued to hold prayer meetings at home, and I'm sure I was on top of their prayer list. My grandmother was particularly upset because she knew Kalle and Jared's clientele being a socialite herself. Tongues were wagging that Kalle was in a scandalous threesome affair with Jared and me! Jared displayed feminine qualities, but I sensed he was too conservative to come out of the closet. Somehow, Kalle was labeled as his boy-toy?

"He's my business partner, nothing to it." Kalle tried to convince me when I confronted him with the rumors. "People get jealous because we run a successful enterprise."

Although I suspected that Jared was totally in love with Kalle, from the dagger-like looks he shot me, I chose to believe Kalle. They were oftentimes invited to all the society parties, when they did show up, they sold diamonds and jewels; Jared was like a jester, he was a society columnist. My relationship with Kalle was getting in Jared's way; I was now a threat to him.

After my graduation, I had to assess my relationship with Kalle. Life was good, but I was getting restless. How many waterfalls can we chase, rivers to run, or jungles to trek? I wanted something more and realized that Kalle had no plans or intention about our future other than *going with the flow*. He was equally disappointed that my family did not support him but in fact, ostracized him. I also suspected Kalle wasn't loyal to me.

When I finally confronted him about his previous affairs, it ripped and shredded my heart into a tiny million pieces.

"There's more facet to our relationship," Kalle rationalized. "Don't make it about this one thing, monogamy. You need to take our entire experience into account. And you must admit, we had one hell of an experience."

"Really?" I retorted and to myself, I said, "The last thing I want is to mimic my parent's marriage. I lived long enough to absorbing my mother's pain."

By then, I knew I was gone and Kalle was my first big heartbreak.

At the end of the day, I could no longer ignore my parent's pain. I didn't want to repeat their mistakes, so I had to make a decision for my life. In as much as I wanted more than the adventures, and in addition the pressure from my parents, my grandmother, my peers, Jared, Kalle's disloyalty, and my future were tormenting me. I withdrew emotionally from the relationship, then physically, and finally I just went back home. Feeling betrayed, Kalle retaliated and distracted himself into the next relationship, setting eyes on other women to soften the blow of the impending doom of our affair.

I needed to go as far away as possible, where he couldn't lure me with a dozen roses, jewelry, or the next big adventure. I crossed the ocean to Manila to work for Dad and to cut the cord. Dad was happy that I came to my senses and welcomed me back with open arms by rewarding me with a home, a job, and a car.

Feeling my pain, Dad consoled me. "There are many fishes in the ocean, love," he said. "You will survive this."

Veering back to Dad's room, I tossed the photo aside, acknowledging that family is indeed everything! My parents had their shortcomings, but they always had my back and wanted what was best for me. This is the true power of unconditional love.

20 RELIVING HISTORY

September 2007

We gathered in the conference room at the library for the last day of our writing class together with my fellow writers and Ralph, our moderator. My heart skipped a beat as published authors and guests stepped inside the room. After several interviews with Dad, I was able to collect my notes and came up with a raw draft. With Ralph's prodding and encouragement, it was my turn to share.

Breaking into a sweat, I approached the podium, gazed at the crowd, glanced at my cheat sheet, then drew in a breath, and read.

Political Prisoner

Despite the tragedy of being taken away from his home and family, my dad's brief time in custody at the Malacañang Palace was comfortable. He and the political prisoners could not have anticipated that within a few weeks, they'd be relocated to the Maximum-Security Unit in Fort Bonifacio with compounds surrounded by barbed-wire fences, searchlights, and guard towers occupied by gun-toting Military Police.

The crowd listened intently as I narrated Dad's story.

The contrast between the palace and the prison was stark with tiny and dim cells.

"I could cross the entire floor in three long strides," Dad had relayed. "Inside the cell was a toilet and a sink. They supplied us with a single bucket of water for all our daily needs—shower, toothbrush, bowels. One pail of water was our ration for the entire day."

But it was the emotional and psychological environment that took the biggest toll on prisoners like my dad. At any time of the day, gunshots would echo off the concrete walls and signify the execution of a fellow prisoner.

Guards would stroll by and taunt and threaten them. "Tomorrow it will be your turn!" Dad and those around him lived each day, not knowing if it would be their last.

Even more, terrifying for the prisoners was to be awakened in the middle of the night, blindfolded, and driven to a cemetery. The political prisoners were lined up, each in front of newly dug graves. The guards spoke menacingly to them about what their fate might be in that graveyard. A rifle was held to their head, or they were given a pistol to shoot themselves like Russian roulette. The prisoners trembled and wept. Some of them lost control of their bowels or and peed in their pants.

The guests opened their eyes wide as I continued to relay Dad's story.

With a gun pointed at his head, Dad closed his eyes, bowed his head in surrender, and whispered a brief prayer, "Lord, please help me." He paused then continued. "If this is my time, may your will be done."

He looked up to the guard and said, "Please let my wife know I am sorry, and that I love her."

A shot pierced the night; a shrill cry escaped his lungs.

"I'm alive," he gasped. "Thank you, Jesus, for another day."

I swallowed hard, acknowledging how difficult it was for Dad.

Some days were long and lazy, but then there were the jolts that came unexpectedly. For no reason, the guards would transfer some of them under solitary confinement known as *'bartolina'*. This meant sunless days that could stretch into months spent alone in a cramped box of a cell. Meager food was slipped under the iron door into the darkness.

"We had to use our hands to eat," my Dad revealed in our interview. "A man could lose his sanity in there." He'd explained that these *blackouts* from the outside world included all news, letters, and visits from loved ones.

"Our meals consisted of dried fish and rice. This didn't bother me at all since I grew up in humble circumstances after I ran away from home," he'd said. "I was used to a simple diet of dried fish, rice, and some vegetables. I was also accustomed to being hungry and hearing the rumblings of my stomach. During this period, there was nothing for me to do but think and ask myself how I got here?"

During the talks I had with him after his release, I not only learned about his experiences as a prisoner but also the details of his childhood and family. Before these discussions, I'd known only a broad outline -the kind of sanitized history that parents tell their young kids. I took careful mental notes as he shared the highs and lows of his upbringing.

The audience inched closer to hear more.

Dad's Story

Dad was born and raised on Comey Island, North of Cebu, an island loaded with a rich mystical culture and heritage. This island contained a legacy of magical mystical beings such as dwarves living in your garden or in the trees; with 'White Lady' sightings from the highway, these were half-bodied witches cruising at night, and preying on the fetuses of pregnant women; St. Elmo's fire graced the coastlines as well as *'Sigbin'* sightings. *Sigbin*s are nocturnal creatures in Filipino mythology believed to appear at night and suck the blood of victims from their shadows.

During the 1600's when Spanish galleon trade from Mexico to the Philippines was rampant, there was a legend that a monsoon caused a shipwreck with no survivors. The ship brought cacao and loads of sweet potatoes, called *camote* and this is how the islands got their name, "Comey" for short. Wide talks about the galleon ship continue to be a topic among the elderly locals to this day.

The Japanese also fled to the island during World War II. Long after the US' victory, Japanese hid inside the caves. Rumors percolated about Yamashita's gold. These were treasures looted by General Yamashita who conquered Malay in seventy days, he concealed it in Comey Island's numerous hidden caves, tunnels, and underwater complexes, since Comey Island is bestowed with an abundance of these natural resources. The island also attracts an influx of treasure hunters especially from Japan, and in present times, tour groups have been organized to explore the rumored hidden treasures the island promises.

Finally, the island is rumored to be a portion of the lost continent of Lemuria. Their ascendants were 'crystal people' who were sharply attuned to nature possessing gifts of heightened intuition. I'd like to believe that I have gifts for *knowing* and *seeing* the future that stem from these roots. For instance, I could tell if someone was going to die.

The crowd knitted their eyebrows in disbelief just begging me to tell them more.

"The Philippines is an ancient country with so much history and folklore." Smiling I addressed their concerns then continued.

I was always fascinated and fixated with the stories of these mystical beings that my *'yayas'* used to share with me before I'd go to bed. I anticipated encounters from these paranormal entities every time I visited. Aside from having a holy grotto in your garden, the locals would also install ceramic dwarves in their garden to honor their real existence. They'd make regular apparitions to a chosen few who were born with the 'third-eye'. The locals would also make a sign of the cross or ask permission to certain trees before breaking their branches or tearing a leaf.

In the 1700s, the Spanish friars introduced Christianity to the *Indios*—natives of the Philippines, and they established churches in most rural part of the island hoping to extinguish their relationship with nature and their homage to other deities. The crossbreed between the Spanish friars and *Indios* produced fair-skinned, *Mestizos*—a racial highbred.

"Let me give you a brief history of my great-grandfather, Arturo Paloma who was a successful entrepreneur and known to run a bazaar that supplied everything the islander needs."

He owned the busiest and largest store in town. Interisland trading was robust, and his bazaar was the epicenter of commerce in the Visayas Island. When people did not have money to buy their necessities, my great-grandfather, accepted portions of their land as promissory notes. After a couple of years, he wound up owning the entire island. He was not only rich but also powerful. The locals voted him to be the '*Barangay Captain*' and his role was designated to sort out every dispute the people had amongst one another. He was able to build a huge mansion in town and when the bell struck every night at six PM, the residents ceased what they were doing and knelt in prayer.

My great-grandfather had two daughters, Mama Lingling and Lola Beatrice. Since they were sent to a private boarding school in Cebu, my grandmother and her sister were frequently shuttled to and from school on their private airplane. If Mama Lingling was not in school, she was playing polo, a hobby afforded only to the local elites as they had a farm that housed a stable of horses.

I learned that my great-grandfather arranged the marriage of my grandparents when my grandmother was just fourteen years old. My grandfather was an eligible bachelor in his late twenties and considered a *catch,* being the only doctor in town, and a most suitable match for my grandmother. Their budding marriage ended abruptly, one stormy night when Dr. Victor Zara hopped on his horse and headed out to treat a patient.

No one knows exactly what happened, though some speculated that a thunderbolt must have frightened the horse, but when they discovered my grandfather, he was unconscious on the ground. His injuries caused him to be bedridden for several days, leaving him in a weakened state. He contracted tuberculosis and died of pneumonia leaving behind his wife, my dad, and his brother, my *Tito* Silvester.

My grandmother, Delilah Paloma Borello (Lingling), inherited her husband's estate and had also received a large bequeath from her father, who through his business acumen accumulated a great deal of property. My grandmother and her sister inherited a vast estate from their parents and were considered the most eligible bachelorettes on the island. Sadly, this was also the cause of their contention. The sisters did not speak to each other for many years until *Lola* Bea's deathbed. Unfortunately, my *Lola* Bea (short for Beatrice) married a conman, who gambled her inheritance away and squandered it on women and wine. She died sick and penniless, while my Mama Lingling was wiser and kept a strict rein on her assets. Mama was able to multiply her wealth, due to her business acumen and frugal habits.

Now I understand why my father always encouraged me and my sister to watch each other's back. A squabble over land originated between the sisters, their misgivings were inherited by their children, and their cousins, and their children's children. To this day, because of disputes a vast portion of that inheritance is inaccessible to the current generation owing to the squabbles which threaten the property's confiscation under the Land Reform Act.

Though she had enough wealth to live on her own, my grandmother (Mama Lingling) remarried a dashing man again, named Fabian Borello. He was of Italian descent and played the piano beautifully. In those days, piano recitals were like rock concerts and when Fabian played the piano, the entire audience was captivated. Consequently, my Lola Lingling was smitten— hook, line and sinker!

Aside from being a concert pianist, Fabian was a talented surgeon and his career made him more attractive to the ladies, especially their elders. Unfortunately, this debonair doctor was already married not only once, but also twice. But Mama Lingling was used to getting what she wanted and was unfazed.

She wound-up marrying him after his previous marriages were annulled, and by him, she welcomed six more children into the fold of our family. My father enjoyed having the half-siblings, but never got along well with his stepfather.

"Every time I defied him; I was disciplined. I remember him throwing a fork at me in one of our flare-ups that scarred me for life!" My dad said.

Indeed, I could still see the faint scar over his upper lip, but I believe he was hurt more from the emotional scars inflicted during that time of his childhood. My Dad said he wondered how anyone could love the man who had become his stepfather; though he was adored by Mama Lingling and by the children they'd had together.

"Even though I came from a prominent family I grew up on the streets, by my own choice," he said.

I guess my dad always missed his biological father. A man he barely knew. "At my lowest ebb," he told me. "I asked Mama, 'Did you ever love my Papa?' and she said no. I wasn't surprised. I think that my brother, Silvester and I were reminders of that life."

By the age of twelve, my dad could not take it anymore. He said his life was *insufferable* and he ran away, finding occasional shelter with relatives on his father's side and with people who once worked on his mother's estate.

"They treated me like a little prince," he said.

But life on the streets was hard and forced him to become a self-made man. He did everything under the sun from selling candies and cigarettes on the streets, polishing shoes, driving *Jeepneys*, even hooking up with elderly married women who nurtured him. He tried anything he could think of to get where he wanted to be.

During the Japanese occupation from 1942, my dad witnessed the Japanese pillage and burning of the villages, torturing the Filipinos, and raping our women. This motivated him to join the guerilla movement in his teens during WWII. He fought alongside the Americans against the Japanese.

My dad hid with the guerillas in the local mountains to evade capture and imprisonment and joined a resistance group. After the war, everything was burned including the schools and their records. "When the war was over, I returned to the city and accelerated myself to a higher grade." Dad admitted, "after all, no documents were disproving it."

For his service as a veteran, my dad was awarded a scholarship. He desired to be a doctor in his heart, but since he did not have the resource to pursue an education in the medical field, he decided to become a civil engineer. I do believe that my dad was destined to be an engineer. He embraced numbers and possessed a photographic memory. I recited a ten-digit phone number one time, and he remembered it immediately. My dad was a math whiz too, maybe this was because he had a Lemurian birthright?

Tangential flashbacks like these are what occupied my dad's mind in those days and weeks spent in solitary confinement in Marcos's prison. For him, there was little sleep and only thoughts and worries to keep him company. This included concerns over the welfare of the employees of the business he was forced to abandon.

We took a short break to eat some snacks before I resumed my story.

My dad started his career as a city engineer, managing projects on the side to accumulate enough money and nurture the necessary political connections to launch his own company. After years of work and savings, he built his own construction business that became known for significant projects such as the first local, large-scale land reclamation project that widened Cebu, in fact he built a bridge that connected Cebu to the smaller island of Mactan.

My dad built his reputation by taking on mega-projects and building roads and bridges throughout the Philippines. By the time of the infamous 1969 election, he was so highly regarded that should Serging have won the presidency, it was almost assured my dad would have been named Minister of Public Works and Highway for the Philippines.

It is no wonder that he fell into a depression and despair as the months of imprisonment wore on and uncertainty prevailed in Fort Bonifacio with no end in sight. "There were days when I couldn't get out of bed," he remembered. "I was at my lowest point in life. I felt forsaken by everyone; by my government, my friends, and even by God himself."

He called upon both his heavenly father and his departed biological father to give him strength and not to leave him there to rot. He also shared with me that in these isolated moments; he would feel a presence, like a soft, gush of wind sweeping over his face. "Father, why have you forsaken me? It was as if a warm, benevolent spirit was there with me and confirming that I was not alone."

After his release from prison, my dad continued to call upon the biological father he'd never really known, and that inexplicable feeling of comfort returned.

Taking a deep breath, I paused and smiled at the audience who were glued to my story. Adrenalin rushed upon me as the guests rose from their seats with a warm-hearted applause. Unsure how my story would be received, goose bumps crawled all over my skin while my heart did somersaults.

I finished, my voice quivering, "I am writing a book about my dad, but little did I know that when writing his story, I discovered a lot about myself. The young, fragile, insecure child has transformed into a confident, daring, and independent woman. Transcribing my dad's life into paper helped me understand myself better as to why I think and act this way. My story is the *Yin*, and my dad's is the *Yang*. Knowing the background and history of my parents and their relationship makes me whole." I teared-up a bit. "For the first time in my life and after running away from all the painful memories that haunted me, I had finally connected the pieces together and chosen to embrace everything—the joys and trials."

Loud clapping filled the air. Wiping my tears before they could start in earnest, I stepped down from the podium feeling like a dark cloud had been lifted.

10 FAMILY PORTRAIT

November 21, 2018

November served to be a significant month for me since aside from Thanksgiving, Mom passed away on November 12 and Dad on November 21 though several years apart. Although Thanksgiving is not a holiday formally celebrated in the Philippines, but we honored it since it was Mom's favorite holiday. She'd always take the opportunity to remind us to be grateful for all things in life whether good or bad.

Since November is when we pay tribute to our parent's life, my husband, my siblings, and their families gathered at our ancestral home to celebrate.

The turkey roasted on an open fire for hours out in the yard, while Edgar basted the skin to make it moist and juicy every 45 minutes. Candy whipped some mashed potatoes as her husband Keith poured milk into the bowl. Armando set the bowl of cranberry sauce on the table.

"Yum, that looks good!" I tried to dip my finger to have a teeny-weeny taste of it, but Armando whisked it away from me.

Manuel arrived with sautéed green beans and rested them on the table. Jake and Giselle, his wife, popped in with a round tray of colorful fancy *Pancit Palabok*.

"Oh, my goodness!" My eyes grew wide. "This may not be considered a traditional Thanksgiving dish, but I'm so glad you brought it, I've been craving it!"

I set the tray on the table.

"It's the most sought-after dish in town and since you've been living abroad, this should satisfy those cravings." Giselle winked.

Jake chimed in, "And as for dessert, we brought some local deli, *Leche flan*, and *Brazo de Mercedes.*"

"Oh my God, you are spoiling us!"

I was thrilled to see my entire family gathered around the dining table, minus Rudy who was most likely playing the guitar in heaven.

"Bless us, oh Lord," Jake led the prayers.

"And these thy gifts," we said in unison.

During our prayer, I peeked at the family oil portrait hung on the wall; it was painted back in the 1970s. I then glanced at my siblings noted how far we've come.

No doubt, my sister Candy and my brothers also struggled. In hindsight, I came to realize we all responded to the same event in various and *damaging* degrees. We all ran, thinking we were running to something when in truth, we were running away from that childhood trauma. However, I can only speak for myself about how our tragedy affected my life, but I tried to understand what each of my siblings dealt with it in their own ways. Though we battled our demons, I think we found many blessings on the road to becoming who we are today. There are many facets to our collective story, but what follows is only my version of how each of my siblings experienced that formative part of our family life.

After saying Amen, Armando, our eldest brother popped the bottle of champagne, filled all our glasses, and toasted to our parents. "Here's to you, Mom and Dad. You both had a unique way of raising us, but in the end, we all turned out okay."

My two older brothers had different experiences of our family than I did since they were already abroad when Dad was arrested. Nonetheless, in my eyes, they were subject to our parents' unique philosophy of sending kids away when they became particularly troublesome even though they might want to leave themselves.

I stared at my brother Armando. He was heavier, with streaks of gray breaking out from his thick jet-black hair. His face displayed confident experience, tired and weary from a stressful job of fighting for the oppressed as a Labor Union Leader. Sipping champagne from the fluted glass, I was in awe of how far he'd changed. This kind, generous, and fair man that I know and love today was quite different in our youth.

As the first-born child, he was showered with attention and indulgence. In the 1960s, when the Beatles and the Monkees were wildly popular, Mom saw to it that Armando had twelve-string guitar and stylish clothes. And when he was kicked out of his private Catholic boys' school for refusing to cut his hair, our parents searched the region for a school that would accept him, long hair, rebellious behavior, and all.

"Hey, Armando," I quipped. "Didn't you hold a grenade in your hand when we were kids scaring the life out of us?"

"C'mon now." Armando blinked. "That grenade was a dud! You don't need to remind me."

"We were all so scared of you and Wella, our cousin would get the runs when she knew you were nearby."

"Why are you talking about this now?" Armando blushed while glancing at his wife, Emma, and the kids.

"I remember! You shared this story with me." Emma squeezed his arm.

"Sorry to bring it up, but I am just so proud of what you have become. Now you are fighting for social justice, the rights of the many oppressed by the powerful few." I clinked his wine glass.

I believe that our pampered lifestyle induced Armando to act as a neighborhood bully at times—a period in his life that he regrets. And it was his oppositional behavior that got Armando a plane ticket to America at the age of fifteen where he started a new chapter in his life.

My parents deemed it as a punishment, although for Armando, it was a *dream come true*. During the 60s he wanted to go to the United States to experience the free-love revolution, the hippie movement, flower power, Woodstock, peace, love, sex, drugs, and rock & roll.

Although he was gone, Dad's arrest forged a path for Armando to make politics a *way of life*. He studied Political Science to make a difference in society. At one time, he tried to reach out to Amnesty International to advocate for Dad's early release. When he graduated from college, he worked as a Labor Union leader in the US and abroad and dedicated his life to fight inequality, injustice, and local and global corruption at all levels.

Manuel, who finished eating his meal, rose from his seat, grabbed the guitar that was displayed in the corner, and strummed to Beatle tunes.

"Here comes the sun…"

Singing along, I was transported back in time when all we did was play the guitar and sing happy songs.

Manuel was playing the same happy tunes forty years ago and after how many decades, he has maintained his physique by playing tennis daily.

"Doesn't our brother look like Charlie Sheen?" My sister Candy asked me, referring to Manuel.

I studied his features. "That's right. There's quite a resemblance."

Though Manuel's demeanor was different compared to Armando's, I thought of him as the personification of the adage, 'Silent waters run deep.' Manuel was a quiet boy, perhaps overshadowed by the outgoing Armando. He was content to play his guitar, sing merry melodies, and cause no grief to the family.

Of course, no teenage boy gets through that stage in his life without some parental strife. I remember the day that Manuel's fate was sealed. He and my mom were engaged in a loud, emotional argument. The last word was from Manuel who cried, "When you're bad, you're sent away. When you're really bad, you get sent abroad!" His sentiments were about his brothers who were already gone.

"Do you remember that day, Manuel?" I asked.

"I am so sorry," Manuel smiled. He said, "I wish I could confirm it for you, but I don't remember it at all."

It makes sense, I blocked out half of my childhood memories because I did not like the implications. Thankfully, a writer can rewrite history and write a better childhood if they liked. No wonder I was drawn to the vocation.

Within days, Manuel was packed and ready to be sent off to Canada. In the meantime, Armando relocated to Seattle, Washington. When Manuel was finally able to join Armando in the U.S.; he settled in Seattle as well.

Manuel was like Dad, he had the *Midas Touch,* meaning everything he touched turned to gold. He was a successful businessman in the US and Cebu investing in land and real estate.

The boys essentially built remarkable futures, absent emotional input, and guidance from our parents.

"Let them fend for themselves," Dad had said when Mom worried about her sons abroad. "You need to throw them in the deep end, so they can learn to swim."

Indeed, they grew up overnight. When Dad was arrested, their allowance stopped and like everyone else in America, Armando and Manuel had to get a job to pursue their college educations and their lives abroad.

"Now, I understand how a servant feels," Armando wrote to us in a postcard, as he worked odd jobs to survive which included a gig working as a janitor.

"Do you care for the breast or the thigh?" Edgar asked, occupied with the roast turkey.

His question jolted me back to the present.

"I prefer the breast please," Jake said.

I glanced at the portrait again and stared at my brother, Jake who was able to maintain his weight by eating right and living a healthy lifestyle. He pumped his body up with exercise and vitamins, he still maintained a fit and lean figure for his age. However, the gray hair with black streaks dominated his head; it was a result of his responsibilities as a high-powered CEO of numerous fortune 500 companies.

"Why didn't you just run Dad's company? You were groomed for the role." I added more rice to my plate.

"Are you kidding me?" Jake carved himself a slice of turkey. "It was too much to handle. I acquired all dad's bad debts, and I was sued left and right. I even had death threats and intimidations to go to prison.

Although Jake suffered many health issues as a child, such as asthma, he pushed himself beyond those challenges in swimming, sports, and chess. On the golf course, Jake was a star, often featured on local and even national news. His seven kids followed in his footsteps, they inherited his drive and ambition, collecting awards in all their various endeavors.

Jake studied business at De La Salle University in Manila and nurtured important connections, preparing to one day take over Dad's business. After graduation, he returned to Cebu to fulfill this destiny. But the business was no longer what he'd expected. Dad had acquired many creditors due to unfinished projects interrupted by his arrest. Jake was swallowed alive by the outstanding debts the company had incurred. Even De La Salle, one of the best high-end prep schools in the country, could not prepare a business graduate for what Jake faced.

"Didn't you join the Krishnas?" I asked.

"Yes, briefly!" Jake sipped his champagne.

As an initiation to the organization, they were required to approach people at the public park and beg for alms. He visited the temple regularly and engaged in Yoga and meditation.

"I remember getting calls from the dead." I crossed my legs.

"What do you mean?" Jake looked confused, munching on a slice of turkey breast.

"Oh, never mind." I gave up. "I must have imagined it."

During this period in his life, we received incessant calls, like a cold voice from the dead looking for my brother. Every time, the phone rang, my sister Candy and I were so scared that we would run upstairs and hide. We refused to answer the phone.

Something was wrong with my brother, as his facial features were riddled with pimples, and he looked like a stranger. To address this problem, my mother brought him home to Cebu and consulted a psychiatrist. In the end, my brother was able to heal with a bombardment of love and prayers from my mother, her prayer group, her church as well as his loving girlfriend, Giselle, who is now his wife.

But until now, I still don't know and understand what happened, was he possessed? Like my secret, it was also a phase in our lives we never talked about.

The maid served the desserts, *Leche flan,* and *Brazo de Mercedes.* I could not help but stare at Rudy's portrait next to mine, and my heart tightened because I was missing Rudy.

"Here's to Rudy." I raised my glass. "To Rudy!" My siblings followed and lifted their glass.

I felt him standing next to me with a glass in his hand, raised it, and could swear I'd heard him say "Cheers!"

Rudy was a charmer. His features were distinctly different from the rest of us, set in an attractive package.

"Were you swapped at birth from your hospital bed?" A friend and relative joke because he had distinct Indian features and did not look a bit like any of us.

Rudy's smile flashed two deeply etched dimples oozing charisma. Rudy was able to penetrate the Mama Lingling iron-clad funds. Mama Lingling was stern and disciplined, particularly when it came to money. She kept a very tight purse, but when Rudy charmed his way into her heart, she opened that purse, again and again, never knowing her generosity was feeding Rudy's demons.

They started to show up shortly before Dad's arrest and continued for most of his life. Rudy was only thirteen years old when he began coming home drunk, often in the company of his drinking buddies. I also remember many times when he'd stumble in the door bearing cuts and bruises, his face and eyes swollen from fights he'd been in. The girls, however, continued to find Rudy attractive and he nurtured the bad boy image. Without my dad's presence and in my mom's frequent absence, there was little supervision or condemnation of Rudy's lifestyle. Even I fell under his spell.

When he exerted his humor and expressed his generosity, people forgave his sins committed in the euphoria of drunkenness. He lived life as if he had no care in the world and dreamed of becoming a rock star. Indeed, Rudy could sing and play his guitar like a pro.

These remarkable characteristics carried Rudy through his adult life, including a thirty-one-year marriage and three remarkable children who were serenaded to sleep with rock and roll tunes since Rudy knew no lullabies. I'm grateful that he found a career as a realtor – self-employment that allowed him to spend time with his kids whose company he deeply valued. His life, however, ended too soon. He died at the age of fifty-five from cirrhosis of the liver.

"Oh my God," I groaned. "I overate again."

They laughed.

The maids served coffee. While stirring my cup and adding cream and sweeteners, I caught a glimpse of the portrait again. I was seated across from Paul who was enjoying the aroma of my coffee; it prompted him to get up and pour himself a cup too.

As he was slicing a piece of *Leche flan,* I studied his face. Paul had lost a lot of weight even though he was living a healthy lifestyle combined with a good diet and regular walks. He underwent a series of complicated and delicate surgeries in Singapore; one to correct what they thought was an intestinal blockage and an earlier gall bladder operation.

Thank you, Lord, that he is alive and is with us today.

"Why did you move out of the house when Dad got back from prison? I probed.

"I did not comply with his lifestyle." Paul shrugged. "Staying in the house would make me complicit."

"Oh!"

While Rudy partied like a rock star, my youngest brother Paul was both scholarly and contemplative. Unlike his older brothers, he had a quiet and thoughtful nature. From early on, he was introspective and preferred spending time with books rather than with people. With his interest in learning and living mainly with his thoughts, Paul was unable to find much support within our household. Our parents had little time to pay attention to Paul's needs for guidance, his interest in schoolwork, and scholarly pursuits. Like our mother, he became absorbed with his faith and became a very dedicated Christian.

Paul had little time for family intrigues and politics. He chose to focus on nature, learning, and forging his path in life. That path allowed him to marry an accomplished woman who became a physician.

"What was your course of study again, Paul?" I asked. "Sorry, I can't keep up."

"No worries," he said. "I just finished my doctorate in Sustainable Development Studies. Now, I am the director of our university department!"

"Congratulations!" I spoke.

"Thanks, but it's just a title really which comes with a lot of duties and responsibilities." He humbly smiled.

"It's still an accomplishment and I bet Mom and Dad would be so proud. We all are!"

"We finally have a doctor in the family. Dad's wish!" Candy chimed in.

More than that, Paul is married to a doctor, Lorna. One of his daughters just wrapped up her internship in the medical field and the two other daughters, intended to pursue a degree in Medicine and follow in their mother's footsteps.

A family of doctors... I smiled. *Dad, you finally have your wish, and you can now rest in peace.*

Armando approached the bar and secured another bottle of champagne. "How about another round?"

"Yes, please." Candy raised her glass closer to Armando. As the bubbles sizzled, I observed my sister then sneaked a look at the portrait again for another quick comparison.

I often think of Candy as a bottle of champagne— bubbly and fun. She is open-minded, non-judgmental, forgiving, and generous. I recall how she loved to dress up, wear sparkling jewelry, and dance for people who visited our home. She exuded a natural feminine beauty while I was the complete opposite and more of a *tomboy*.

Candy, who is a year younger than me had her way of responding to the fate that knocked on our family door, the day my dad was arrested. As the only girls in the house, we received a different kind of treatment than our brothers did. We were encouraged to stick together, and on the other hand, we were pitted against each other. Both our parents engaged in this sometimes-confusing style of raising daughters. We were supposed to be looking after each other while competing for who was prettier, and who was smarter.

The expectations and treatment of girls in families were different in those days, with so much emphasis on appearance from Mom, and the importance of an appropriate marriage by Dad's standards. When things got testy between us, we would each disappear into separate rooms and shut the doors, wanting to be worlds apart; in other moments we were stuck like glue with no distance between us at all.

All of this was designed to protect us because we were girls; however, with all we'd been through with Dad's arrest and Mom's absence to care for her, at age fifteen, Candy chose to escape the family situation. She ran away from home, first going to nuns from her school's convent, and was later *adopted* by a family who were generous donor of the convent. When she was about sixteen years old, she built on her love of dance and joined a dance troop, traveled to Japan, and performed in cultural programs.

I know that Candy went through this period in her life just as I did - running, searching, and suffering. We were compelled to flee—to be somewhere, anywhere else but home.

Because we were both traumatized, we developed a gift that I call our *superpower.*

"I could leave my body in an instant. I can be out of my body and see everyone below me including myself," My sister claimed. "This happens to me a lot, but now I can control it."

"I black out frequently," I said. "I don't remember where I've been."

When this happens to me, I'd say "Ooops, sorry I was out again," I said.

We'd compare notes and then we'd laugh at each other because it was both painful and funny, a secret we both shared and in fact a secret many survivors share.

Ironically, our lives apart paralleled one another. We both ran as far away as we could, married, had a child, and got divorced. Years later, without the pressure to compete, with our many demons silenced, our bond of renewed sisterhood had proved to be the foundation of our relationship. *We are best friends.*

While everyone was catching up, there was a knock on the door, and Arbie, our half-brother appeared.

"Hey, Arbie. Good to see you." I rose from my seat and hugged him. "Thank you for coming."

"It's good to see you!" Arbie smiled.

The rest of my siblings stood up to greet him with a handshake or a hug.

"Grab a seat." I handed him a plate.

Given our father's relationships with other women, I am aware of other siblings related to us, but outside of our nuclear family. I have no doubt they harbor their own memories of the dad who occasionally appeared in their lives. As part of our collective heritage, I respect their privacy and their memories and recount only those events as I experienced them in the Zara household.

Although Arbie's face was missing in the Zara family portrait, Dad was open about his existence. He was born in the same year as our youngest brother Paul. He looks very much like Dad, even now that he was older. Arbie, like dad, pursued a degree in Civil Engineering. We love and accept Arbie as one of us. None of this was his fault.

Shortly before midnight, I raised my glass. "Thank you, everyone, for being here." Then looking above, I added. "To Mom and Dad, we love and miss you. Happy Thanksgiving!"

"To Rudy as well." Armando added.

"Cheers." We all clinked our glasses for a toast to conclude the evening and our memorable family reunion.

Little did we know that what happened to our family was part of an era that would one day appear in history books and reside on the World Wide Web. Despite the disruption in our family life, the children of Mateo and Heike Zara have mostly landed on our feet. Among us are a prominent labor leader, a successful real estate broker, a respected businessman, and a scientist. The Zara siblings gather often, finding each other in the various places we've called home to acknowledge our shared past and affirm our family's mutual commitment to each other.

When I look back at our family as a nucleus, I see it as dynamic parts that collided, joined, fell apart, sped away, and reunited again. Everyone was in constant motion. Becoming attached to places and people proved to be difficult. They are both blessings and curses in that history. But we all learned to survive, to grow, and to thrive.

10 REARVIEW MIRROR

May 2019

After decades of living abroad and running away from my past, I moved back home to Moalboal, the Southern part of Cebu with my current husband, Edgar who is a loving artist and my soulmate. Edgar is medium built, stocky, with hazel brown hair and eyes. He possessed the most charming smile, which never failed to melt my heart. He is also soft-spoken, and I fell in love with his brilliant mind. I thought about retiring and renting a tiny beach cottage to write my book in Comey Island and just when I was at the brink of giving up on love, Edgar came along.

After being together for many years, we created a life for ourselves, close to nature where our creative juices flowed. Some people dreamed about white picket fences, a huge house with a yard, children, and pets, amidst a rainbow backdrop. But my husband and I, along with our Yorkie pups chose a life next to the ocean where we could swim with turtles and sardines, and watch some whales, as well as dolphins, performing their acrobatics in the morning while we have coffee at the porch. We don't mind the crabs crawling in our garden, nor the lizards dropping from the roof, sometimes they fall right into our coffee cups. I didn't realize, lizards love coffee.

Moving to Moalboal, a beach community was one of the best decisions we made.

In our living room overlooking the ocean, I stared at the pile of boxes I had to unearth and sighed, *Oh gee, when will I get done?*

I opened one box and saw a scrapbook my daughter Tara created for me. Tears spilled from my eyes as a thousand needles pricked my heart. *If only I could turn back time.*

I could hear Dad saying the same thing too, repeatedly. As I flipped through the scrapbook, there were baby pictures of Tara and her dad—a family I could have had. My heart broke open again, reliving the raw emotions from those times.

I understand more now how I chose my past relationships. I met my first husband when I was twenty-two years old and working in Manila. Charlie was in Cebu traveling the world and free of all possessions other than his backpack. He was born in Frankfurt, Germany, and enjoying life on the island with no responsibilities. I met him during a short visit home and was quickly swept away—We were a match.

No one in my circle of friends understood the attraction I felt for Charlie and his lifestyle. They assumed I'd find a partner with political and social connections—at the very least, a suit-wearing expatriate with advanced education and a job in a multi-national corporation. But here I was, head over heels falling for a beach bum whose only plan was to enjoy himself wherever he roamed. I believed he was my ticket out of Cebu, while he thought he found his ticket to Cebu. He was another runner with bigger dreams than mine.

But a challenge emerged as we made plans to conquer the world and fulfill our biggest dreams Charlie fell in love with my island and wanted nothing more than to live on the beaches of Cebu.

"Anywhere but Cebu!" I debated. "Look, we have 7,100 islands to choose from."

I acknowledged that my youthful adventures aggravated my parents as they tried to rebuild their own lives. Mom was engulfed in her Christian ministry and prayer groups while Dad recaptured his social stature.

Dad took me aside and gave me some advice. "Listen, don't smear our family name. Whatever you need to do, just do it on a different island."

"Come move with me to Manila," I asked Charlie, heeding my fathers' warnings.

Manila was a big city with a wider population we could live anonymously, without desecrating my father's last name.

"I don't like Manila, if you want me to live in a big city, it would have to be Frankfurt."

Charlie convinced me that it would be an opportunity for me to know his family, his country, and his language. I agreed, since Germany was a world away from the Philippines, maybe far enough for me to bury my past and make a future.

In Germany, I was greeted with open arms by Charlie's family who was deeply grateful that I returned their prodigal son to them. He left his country two years prior and fled to remote places to live in the image of his literary hero, *Robinson Crusoe.* Even as we settled in Frankfurt, we were both filled with wild and ill-defined plans for our lives. I presumed Charlie was a backpacker with few resources, but when we moved to Germany, I learned he was from a well-off family with real estate and business interests.

Six months after our arrival in Frankfurt, Charlie and I were proud owners of United Fitness Club in Frankfurt boasting more than a hundred members. It was originally a boxing and karate club that the owner, John sold to us to pursue his dream of becoming a movie star in Hollywood. We turned the club into a family-oriented fitness center with weight machines and offered dance courses, martial arts, yoga, and aerobics, riding the wave of a fitness cult inspired by Jane Fonda in the 1980s and the excitement over aerobics.

Dance music bounced off the walls from the gym on the second floor. Men and women gyrating to 80s disco workout music, working up a sweat as their breath fog the mirror in a temperature of -10 degree Celsius, as we opened the window to air it out.

Downstairs was a vitamin bar made of rustic oak, serving protein shakes, health bars, and freshly pressed fruit shakes, to pumped up muscled men and women who delighted in torturing themselves as they attacked the circuit machines. MTV and music of the eighties resonated in the building, as the plants danced and thrived from the carbon dioxide expelled from everyone's breath and steam from their working bodies.

Grateful for the kindness and hospitality of Charlie's parents, we invited them to have dinner at a restaurant. His father, Gerhardt, wore a suit, had piercing blue eyes and possessed a loud booming voice that hinted his dominant character while he ordered wine menu. His beautiful, elegant wife, Uschi who was all jeweled up with priceless family heirloom studied the menu, looking every inch like the actress Gina Lollobrigida with her hazelnut wavy hair and double D bosom.

We ordered several *aperitifs* and our favorite dish, *Duck a l'orange.*

"What is the celebration for?" Gerhard asked.

As the steaming duck was served on the table, after we had our first round of *aperitifs*, Charlie blurted. "We also have a duck in the oven."

Their eyes widened, jaws dropped, and they cheered, *"Herzliche Glückwünsch!"*

Ecstatic with the news of a new addition to the family, they rose from their seats and gave us big hugs. Gerhard could not sleep and was making plans around the birth of his first granddaughter, as to what school she'd go to, so forth, and so on. Uschi was pondering over a variety of names.

Although it was Charlie's dream to own his restaurant and needed only the capital of DM 40,000. His father, the financier had bigger dreams and released DM 500,000.00 at very minimal interest to ride the wave of the Fitness World. It was his dream initially to invest in Fitness Clubs with pools and tennis courts.

They helped us settle in our family life and business. A child signaled our intention to integrate with a conventional lifestyle, and that naturally meant we needed a steady source of income. Charlie's father, a successful businessman, loaned us money to set up a business, even though neither one of us had the essential experience or expertise to handle it. Charlie was the apple of his father's eye, but he was also a savvy businessman. So, in lending us the money, he was able to get an inheritance tax break, while supporting his family at the same time.

We rode the swell for nearly eight years, but things went South as we accumulated a mountain of debt and blamed each other for the collapse of our business. Not even Tara who was the glue of our marriage could save us. We both opted out of the business and the marriage.

I was a single mom in a foreign country, juggling three jobs to pay the bills and leaving my daughter in the care of others. I felt an overwhelming urge to run again—from motherhood and myself. I was so depressed and so naïve. In the Philippines, it's not unusual for parents to leave their children with relatives while trying to rebuild financial security, but this is not nearly as common in Germany. I didn't think that these decisions were permanent, and I didn't think I would lose Tara.

Will I ever be whole again? What am I looking for? What do I want in life?

Besieged with these questions, I thought long and hard while waiting for my flight, and then wrote Tara this letter.

To my dearest darling daughter,

You may not understand why I left, but someday when you are older you will know that I love you very much with all my heart and more than my life, but I need to do this for myself.

The truth will set us free,

Mom

Goodbye my darling, goodbye Frankfurt! My heart broke and frayed into a million fragmented shards.

Leaving Tara with her father was painful for me, but I was overwhelmed, clinically depressed and desperate finding myself lost amid confusion, chaos, and fear. I also needed to rebuild and heal my financial, emotional, and mental health.

I couldn't figure out how life worked and there was no manual or encyclopedia on how to deal with divorce, or how to raise a child alone in a foreign country. I only knew how to run. My daughter was growing up fast, but if I stayed, I could have killed myself as I was already on the way to self-destruction—*Sex, Drugs, and Rock & Roll.* I was toxic and needed to keep Tara away from me while I sorted things out searching for the truth and finding myself. The irony of all of it is, that I left Tara at the same tender age I was when my dad was taken prisoner. She was the ultimate sacrifice, a decision that torments me to this very day.

After running away from my problems and responsibilities, I spent time in Chile and got involved with Pablo, a charmer who had a chiseled face, round eyes with the thickest lashes. My Chilean escapade left me flat in my face since Pablo betrayed me and got my friend pregnant.

I could have taken the first flight back to Frankfurt, but here I was alone now, with no country, no family, no husband, and no daughter. My pride was all I had, and I refused to yield to my downfall. I couldn't imagine going back to Frankfurt, so I chose to stay in another foreign country to seek life by myself, a clean slate. During my three-year stint in Chile, I traveled a lot to the US, India, Germany, Peru, and the Philippines keeping myself busy and not wanting to confront my failures or regrets. In the pursuit of finding myself, distractions and chaos filled the empty void and numbed the pain.

I thought my life would fall into place and I would reunite with my daughter so we could be together again even if it was just, she and I, but life is always a mystery and sometimes life is unkind. Things don't always go the way you we'd want. Dad was always there to rescue me during the lowest points of my life. Although he reminded me that these were consequences to my actions, it was always done with love and compassion.

I was never able to recapture those years and recreate a family for Tara and me, she still graces my life with her beauty and brilliance. Our yearly reunions help make up for the lost time and we have found room for healing and forgiveness.

The puppies barked announcing their presence and broke my reverie. Too much nostalgia drains my life. I closed the album and set it aside in time for *Happy Hour.*

Edgar popped in with a glass of margarita and a bag of tortillas. "Hi, honey."

"Perfect, I was just craving for that. Thank you, love." I gave him a peck on the lips.

We nestled in a sweet embrace and allowed ourselves to get lost at the moment while watching the sunset.

23 COMING HOME

November 2019

A flock of birds surged above me and settled on the grounds of what used to be our ancestral home. Like an outsider, I stood at the guardhouse frozen in time and disbelief as traces of our childhood obliterated before my eyes. Our house was razed to the ground and replaced with ten townhouses tucked in a small compound. Armando was fortunate to buy one of the units from the developer and picked the spot where my parents' room was previously located. With his key, I marched inside the empty townhouse hoping to feel a tinge of Mom and Dad's presence and the heartbeat of our home, but instead fresh paint and new tiles replaced my nostalgia.

I peered outside the window to what used to be the tennis court, but instead of hearing bouncing balls, an empty lot stared right back at me. With eyes shut, I visualized an image of the twelve-year-old innocent girl sobbing in pain as she begged the soldiers not to arrest her father. Strong raw emotions surged all over my body as goosebumps broke out on my skin.

Opening my eyes, I acknowledged that the feelings now were just as strong as fifty years ago.

***

That afternoon, after celebrating our annual reunion with my brothers and sister, we visited Dad's grave at the Golden Haven in Consolacion, Cebu. Yellow bells were scattered, candles were lit, and everyone bowed down in prayer.

After the solemn prayers, my siblings proceeded to the pavilion to quench their thirst and sought refuge from the scorching sun while I squatted on the grass facing Dad's grave. Although Mom was buried in Concord, California, I know she and Dad are together.

I seized a book from my handbag and held it up high. "To Dad, this is our family saga—*Shards of Time*. We did it, Dad! The years you suffered in prison were not in vain, this is your legacy—our legacy for the many generations to come."

Posing for a selfie with my book, I continued to tell Dad how much I appreciated him. "Dad, you did not only build roads, bridges, buildings, reclamation parks, and cemeteries but you build us a wonderful home with fond memories where love lives and thrives unshakeable through the passage of time. And you did all that, your way."

As if an answer to my monologue, I heard the tune of "My Way" from the background. *My Dad's National Anthem.*

Yes, there were times I'm sure you knew,

When I bit off more than I could chew

But through it all, when there was doubt,

I ate it up and spit it out. I faced it all and I

stood tall and did it my way.

After saying goodbye to Dad, I reminded myself that home is not determined by the time and place, but where your heart is. Edgar approached me with a bottle of ice-cold refreshing water, and then pulled me up from the ground.

We locked in a tight embrace. "Thanks, love, let's go home."

An orange monarch butterfly landed on my shoulder as the cool breeze swept over my skin. With a smile etched on my face, I gazed at the clear, blue sky while my heart soared with *hope.*

EPILOGUE

My family's history is just a minor page in the larger story created by the Marcos regime. Indeed, there are thousands of stories like ours, and many are much more deeply tragic. I feel that it's especially relevant today because of the reemergence of autocratic governments all over the world, and being in the Philippines now, with the anti-terrorist bill implemented, I can't help but see it as a sign of autocratic dictatorship, although in a modified version—Martial Law 2.0. Dad was set free on the condition that he would not engage in political activities but staying silent makes us complicit.

I state my truth, it's *No To Dictatorship.*

#NeverAgain.

Our family saga is a tale of financial and personal loss that forever changed the trajectory of the Zara family. I have recorded this personal experience so future generations will be able to peek inside the tragedy we endured and the events that shaped our family during the Martial Law era. But more than anything, this story is about a young girl, Mita who lost her youth. Her goal was to unravel the myth behind her name and to reveal her true purpose in life.

As I continue to navigate through this journey called life, I've learned that lightning never announces when it will strike, and I've realized how everything can change in an instant. While I chose to run far away from my childhood home to escape crushing inner demons, through traversing a bumpy and zigzag road, I've come to understand that life is never black and white— in between there will always be shades of grey. Instead of running away, I've decided to embrace the good and the bad, which led me to find my true purpose that binds our family together—*FORGIVENESS.*

#FamilyIsEverything

#ForgiveToHeal

CEBU

Island of my birth,
Mother Earth. Clear blue skies
reflect glistening pristine seas and mountains,
warm humid sticky air, hot and dry.
Gentle, friendly, carefree people
who talks in a song, makes me feel blue
makes me long…

I ran away from you all the time

seeking greener pastures in a foreign land.

You lure me back to you
through nostalgia and melancholy

Every time I return
reality streams deeper in my veins
that I belong to you
and you belong to me.

Be still my heart,
There's nowhere else to run,
but the journey within.

It has become clear,
above everything I hold dear
that you will always be a part of me
etched in the deepest recesses of my psyche

GLOSSARY

Adobo – A signature Filipino dish that involves meat, seafood, or vegetables marinated in vinegar, soy sauce, garlic, bay leaves, and black peppercorns, which is browned in oil, and simmered in the marinade.

Aperitifs – Appetizer

Asa ka mo Adto? – Where are you going?

Ate – Older sister

Barangay captain - Chairman of a town

Batik – Tie Dye clothing

Bartolina – Dungeon

Bulalo – Boiled soup comprised of beef shanks with bone marrow inside the bone.

Boquerones – Fresh anchovies marinated in vinegar, olive oil, and minced garlic.

Brazo de Mercedes – A traditional Filipino meringue roll with a custard filling typically dusted with powdered sugar.

Callos – A rich stew made of beef tripe, ox feet, Chorizo de bilbao, garbanzo beans, green peas and bell peppers slow-cooked in a paprika-infused tomato sauce.

Camote – Sweet potato

Chica' – slang. An affectionate term of a young girl or woman.

Chokolate – Chocolate drink

Danggit – Dried fish

Dios ko – My God

Duck a l'orange – Duck in Orange Sauce

Empanadas – Pockets of dough that have meat filling. Dough is usually baked or fried consisting of pastry and filling.

Ensaymada – Soft, sweet, dough Filipino pastry similar to a French Brioche Bread which is light and fluffy and rich in egg and butter.

Friseur – Hairstyle

Gi-atay – Damned

Haute Couture – High end fashion

Herzliche Gluckwunsche – Congratulations

Indios – Natives

Jeepneys – A public transportation in the Philippines.

Kanusa ka pauli? – When are you coming home?

Leche Flan – A dessert made-up of eggs and milk with a soft caramel on top.

Lola - Grandmother

Lumpia – Filipino spring roll

Mano – An "honoring-gesture" used in Filipino culture performed as a sign of respect to elders and as a way of requesting a blessing from the elder.

Maayo – Good

Manang or Nang' – older sister

Manoy – Older brother

Mangayo ko ug tabang – We need help.

Merienda – Afternoon snack

Mestiza/Mestizo – People of mixed native Filipino and any foreign ancestry.

Misua soup – Thin salted noodles made from wheat flour and eggs combined with ground pork.

Mungo - Green gram, beans

Nada – Nothing

Noche Buena – Derived from the Spanish word referring to the night before Christmas or Christmas Eve celebration.

Oi – Hey

Oma - Grandmother

Oo – Yes

Pakawanen nak kadi – I'm sorry.

Pancit – Filipino noodles made of egg or rice with an assortment stir fry vegetables and meat.

Pancit Palabok – Noodle in shrimp sauce

Pasalubong – Present

Pesteng yawah – Devil be damned

Pinaskuhan – Christmas gifts

Poblacion - Town

Puto – Rice cake

Queso de Bola – An aged, semi-hard Edam cheese from the Netherlands which is traditionally served with slices of jamón (ham) during Noche Buena.

Sari-sari store – Variety store

Si - It's

Sigbin – Known as a creature in Philippine mythology believed to appear only at night to suck the blood of victims from their shadows.

Sigue lang – It's okay.

Sigue na – C'mon

Suka – Vinegar

Super-balita – Super news

Tagalog – Philippines National Language

Tito – Uncle

Tita – Aunt

Tulong – Help

Tableya – Local chocolate

Tabang - Help

Tubo – Grow

Yaya – Nanny

Zara Kami – We are for Zara.

ACKNOWLEDGMENTS

Dad ~ We started this book project together, and you freely shared memories and information even though I know it may have caused you some pain. Now, a decade later, we have two books to hold in our hands. I believe that you, even after your passing, continued to work with me and guided this book to completion. We did it, Dad. You have been my inspiration.

Mom ~ I misunderstood you, my whole life. You are the epitome of goodness, a hard act to follow, so I did everything in my power to not be like you. But as I grow older, I am grateful to be more like you, although I can never be your equal. Thanks for all your prayers. I never believed in them, but I felt protected by your incantations and now believe that it is you who kept me safe and brought me home.

Darwin ~ Thanks for all your love and support and belief in this book project. Thank you for being my sounding board, suggesting ideas and positive feedbacks. Thank you for helping me with the awesome cover. You rock, you are my world!

Tifani ~ "What will my daughter think of me?" This was always the question that prevented me from going over the edge. Although you probably never felt it, you were my moral compass. Every breath and step that I took in my journey, I always thought of you, and your future with the deepest love. Thank you for having faith in me and trusting in the greater purpose of our journeys, however painful.

Conni ~ My one and only dearest sissie, my biggest fan and supporter. Thank you. I love you more than you ever know. I got your back!

My siblings: Alonzo, Jun-Jun, Butch, Randy, Conni, and Peter ~ Thank you for trusting me in the process of sharing our stories, those that remain in my heart, those that I chose to bury, and those that I recreated for my *happy endings.* Thank you for your belief and encouragement in this project. I love you all.

Darby ~ Thank you for helping me put out and organize the skeletons from the closet. Our original book made it possible for me to put the layers of flesh back on the skeleton. From you, I have learned a lot, the process and journey of publishing a book. I am profoundly grateful!

Geraldine ~ Thank you for believing in me and taking on this project. Thank you for helping me flesh out the skeleton as well as spicing them up. You help me immensely transition from a writer to a storyteller. Thanks again for seeing this book through fruition, with your loving and professional guidance.

To my Yorkie Pups: Zorro, Mei-Mei, and Juju, for hovering around me in the early dawn and keeping me company while I pound on the computer for my story. Your presence made it possible and worthwhile.

ABOUT THE AUTHOR

MITOS SUSON

Mitos Suson has lived in Europe, South America, and the United States. "A Doorbell, A Dictator, A Dad" is her debut Memoir and a healing journey that reflects her tumultuous childhood, the impact of her father's arrest as a political detainee, and the disintegration of her sheltered and privileged family life during the Martial Law era in the Philippines. She graduated with a Bachelor of Arts degree, major in History. After many decades of living abroad, Mitos has returned to her roots in Cebu and during the pandemic, she produced her second book, a fictionalized Memoir based on true events, "Shards of Time."

Check me out here : www.mitossuson.com

Follow me:

FB: https://www.facebook.com/martiallawchild

IG: https://www.instagram.com/ming7210/

Twitter: https://twitter.com/ming7210

If you love memoirs, join the

We Love Memoirs Group: https://www.facebook.com/groups/welovememoirs/

You'll get a warm welcome!

A DOORBELL, A DICTATOR, A DAD

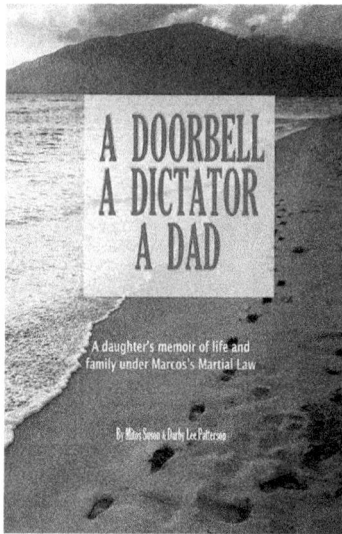

In the 1960s and 70s Ferdinand Marcos ruled the Philippine Islands with the closed fist of a dictator. Families lived in fear, dissenters, political rivals and troubles makers were tossed into Manila's Fort Bonifacio Prison to face an uncertain fate. This is the memoir of one such family, torn apart and scattered asunder when Marcos' henchmen knocked on the door of their home and swept away their father, forever altering their fortunes and future.

Get your copy here.

https://www.amazon.com/dp/B0894QYFB7

Reviews:

Top reviews from the United States

I loved this book and could not put it down! I instantly identified with the author and literally could feel every emotion and event as if I was the one living it!

Much of this story revolves around a singular traumatic childhood event when a little girl from a happy and prominent family lost her dad when who she had considered a very close family friend came with other men to take her daddy away for interrogation for being part of the resistance to the Marcos Regime.

This was during an 8-year period in the seventies and eighties. The traumatic event coupled with the loss of life and lifestyle as she knew it was forever changed for the worse. Her mother checked out emotionally after that, eventually abandoning her all together. All the siblings reacted differently to the event and the complete separation of the family unit.

The author faced life and its struggles largely alone, coming to many realizations on her journey.... but the most important was that she had been running from her past and the emotions tied to it.... I do not want to give away anymore, than that, so I will just say great book, well written, and I have nothing but respect and love for Mitos Suson and I am so grateful she shared her story!

~Lisa Jo Symonds

A Doorbell A Dictator A Dad is a daughter's memoir of life and family under Marcos's Martial Law, by Mitos Suson and Darby Lee Patterson. Marco's refers to President Marcos of the Philippines in the 1970's when he instilled Martial Law.

Growing up in an opulent lifestyle due to her father's business dealings and political connections, Suson's life was forever changed when a close family friend came to detain her father as a political prisoner.

Suson, writes about the struggles she endured as a preteen trying to navigate life under the shadow of her father's arrest, and her mother moving out of the home to be closer to her husband.

The details of the unrest during this time in the Philippines are interesting and scary as she gives the reader firsthand insight into the operation of Martial Law.

~Lori Yerxa

I just finished A Doorbell, A Dictator, A Dad, and I highly recommend. Have you ever heard of a backyard swimming pool that has a tunnel and goes inside the house? If not, get ready! The author weaved the tale of her life in the Philippines with their large family and the antics that go along with having many brothers and sisters. I learned quite a bit about the culture, martial law and traditions. The story unfolded to include heartbreak, laughter, unity and memorable family dynamics.

I LOVE the moment the title of a book makes sense- and this one didn't disappoint.

Beachgirl

See more reviews here:

www.amazon.com/dp/B0894QYFB7#customerReviews

Have you written your review yet?

How Reviews Help Authors

- Many readers decide to read a book based on its reviews. Your review is your recommendation!
- After 20-25 reviews, Amazon includes a book in its "also bought" and "you might like" lists. This increases a book's visibility.
- After 50 to 70 reviews, Amazon selects books for spotlight positions and its newsletter. This provides an enormous boost in visibility and resulting sales!

If you loved a book, please leave a review. It is your gift to the author!

Reviews matter!

It's your gift to the Author.

CPSIA information can be obtained
at www.ICGtesting.com
Printed in the USA
LVHW082122110821
695091LV00011B/290

9 781087 969923